Grapevine

DAILY QUOTE

Book

365 inspiring passages from the
pages of AA Grapevine

Books Published by AA Grapevine, Inc.

Grapevine

DAILY QUOTE

Book

365 inspiring passages from the
pages of AA Grapevine

AAGRAPEVINE,Inc.
New York, New York
WWW.AAGRAPEVINE.ORG

AA PREAMBLE

Alcoholics Anonymous is a fellowship of
men and women who share their experience,
strength and hope with each other that
they may solve their common problem and
help others to recover from alcoholism.

The only requirement for membership is
a desire to stop drinking. There are no
dues or fees for AA membership; we are self-
supporting through our own contributions.
AA is not allied with any sect, denomination,
politics, organization or institution;
does not wish to engage in any controversy,
neither endorses nor opposes any causes.

Our primary purpose is to stay sober
and help other alcoholics to achieve sobriety.

WELCOME

This book captures the first 365 days of the
Grapevine Daily Quote, which first appeared
in June 2012. The quotes—contributed
by AA members, with many written by our
co-founders —were selected by the Grapevine
staff. All of these passages first appeared
in the pages of Grapevine as part of
members' stories and other submissions,
and many of them can now be found
in Grapevine's themed book anthologies.
Each daily quote is accompanied by the
title of the story it came from, the original
issue date and the geographical location
of its writer. Listed at the bottom of each
page is the Grapevine book in which the
quote can also be found.

We hope that you will enjoy these passages
of experience, strength and hope and bring
them into your daily life.

JANUARY

JANUARY 1

"You're Welcome Here"

TULSA, OKLAHOMA, APRIL 1988

———

"If you want to stop drinking
AA doesn't care whether you are
a Christian, a Buddhist, a
Jew, a Mohammedan, an atheist,
an agnostic, or whatever. The
door to AA is wide. Come right in."

———

From *Spiritual Awakenings*

JANUARY 2

"Slow Learner"

MIAMI, FLORIDA, MARCH 1962

———

"All I had to do was ask myself
a simple question: 'Am I or am I
not powerless over alcohol?' I didn't
have to compare myself or my
experience with anyone, just answer
a simple question."

———

From *Step By Step*

JANUARY 3

"The Spiritual Angle of AA"

REV. SAMUEL M. SHOEMAKER
PITTSBURGH, PENNSYLVANIA, OCTOBER 1955

———

"It is when you let truth go into action, and hurl your life after your held conception of truth, that things start to happen."

———

JANUARY 4

"A Candle of Hope"
CLEVELAND, OHIO, APRIL 1991

"The road to spiritual and emotional
recovery ... has taken diverse
routes—lots of meetings, readings,
talks with AA members,
discussion groups, psychotherapy,
and the beginning of sharing.
The keys seemed to be listening and
sharing—the spirit at work."

From *Spiritual Awakenings*

JANUARY 5

"What a Spiritual Awakening Means to Me"

JACKSON HEIGHTS, NEW YORK, APRIL 1956

———

"Ever fresh in my heart is
a song of thanksgiving for my
expanding sobriety, as the
opening door to timeless truth."

———

From *Spiritual Awakenings*

JANUARY 6

"Eye of the Hurricane"

OKLAHOMA CITY, OKLAHOMA, DECEMBER 1992

———

"AA is spiritual, is the eye of the hurricane, is my refuge and my comfort. ... Thanks to AA for making a place for broken hearts and wounded souls."

———

From *Spiritual Awakenings*

JANUARY 7

"Why Alcoholics Anonymous Is Anonymous"

AA CO-FOUNDER, BILL W., JANUARY 1955

———

"We now fully realize that 100 percent personal anonymity before the public is just as vital to the life of AA as 100 percent sobriety is to the life of each and every member."

———

From *The Language of the Heart*

JANUARY 8

"Attitude Adjustment"
NEW YORK, NEW YORK, JANUARY 2006

———

"Not picking up a drink creates infinite possibilities for me. ... Who knows? This could be the greatest day of my life."

———

From *Beginners' Book*

JANUARY 9

"Turning On the Power"

RIVERSIDE, ILLINOIS, AUGUST 1977

———

"The Steps will speak to my condition
wherever I am in sobriety."

———

From *Spiritual Awakenings*

JANUARY 10

"AA and the Religious Turnoff"

NEW YORK, NEW YORK, SEPTEMBER 1977

———

"I realized that it is possible to believe in a Higher Power, in the efficacy of prayer and meditation, in making a conscious contact with a Higher Power as those concepts, privately understood—or not understood—are suggested in AA, without the loss of one iota of my precious identity."

———

From *Spiritual Awakenings*

JANUARY 11

"Let's Keep It Simple—But How?"

AA CO-FOUNDER, BILL W., JULY 1960

———

"We organize our principles merely so
that they can be better understood,
and we continue so to organize
our services that AA's life-blood can
be transfused into those who
must otherwise die. That is the all-in-
all of AA's 'organization.' There
can never be any more than this."

———

From *The Language of the Heart*

JANUARY 12

"The Spiritual Kind of Thirst"

LOS ANGELES, CALIFORNIA, AUGUST 1965

———

"I don't believe I drank to get
drunk, but always to seek in
the next drink that peace for which
a sick soul seems to thirst."

———

From *Spiritual Awakenings*

JANUARY 13

"Unity Seldom Means That We All Agree"

SPRINGVILLE, UTAH, JANUARY 1998

———

"Unity seldom means that we all agree on everything. Nor is unity served by setting aside our concerns and conforming to the majority opinion (or the vocal minority). ... Unity is best achieved by a full hearing of all points of view ... time for all of those involved to step back from emotional responses ... as well as careful consideration and prayer for that which will best serve the group or AA as a whole."

———

From *I Am Responsible*

JANUARY 14

"A Candle of Hope"
CLEVELAND, OHIO, APRIL 1991

———

"Every day, hopeless, helpless alcoholics walk into AA meetings, grab onto hope, and begin a renewal of their spirit."

———

From *Spiritual Awakenings*

JANUARY 15

"Journey of the Spirit"
ALBUQUERQUE, NEW MEXICO, APRIL 1984

———

"I am grateful that the people in AA showed me how to live sober. However, I have learned many things from other sources. I learned about quiet from the breeze floating through the grass on a warm summer day. I have learned unconditional love from my animals. I have learned how to have wonder of the world from my children. I have learned that all things have tremendous power."

———

From *Spiritual Awakenings*

JANUARY 16

"Conscious Contact"

WEST SPRINGFIELD, MASSACHUSETTS, APRIL 1990

———

"The God I know today ...
is a presence in which I find
myself, just as I am."

———

From *Spiritual Awakenings*

JANUARY 17

"At Home in a Home Group"
NEW YORK, NEW YORK, MAY 1997

———

"My drinking career was all about running away. I could pack up and vanish in a flash. Now ... I'm taking the risk to stick around, to just show up and see what happens."

———

JANUARY 18

"Learning to Handle Sobriety"
CONNECTICUT, MARCH 1975

———

"AA does not teach us how to handle our drinking; it teaches us how to handle our sobriety."

———

From AA Grapevine

JANUARY 19

"'Rules' Dangerous but Unity Vital"

AA CO-FOUNDER, BILL W., SEPTEMBER 1945

"When we AAs look to the future, we must always ask ourselves if the *spirit* which now binds us together in our common cause will always be stronger than those personal ambitions and desires which tend to drive us apart. ... Though the individual AA is under no human coercion, is at almost perfect personal liberty, we have, nevertheless, achieved a wonderful unity on vital essentials. For example, the Twelve Steps of our AA program are not crammed down anybody's throat. They are not sustained by any human authority. Yet we powerfully unite around them because the truth they contain has saved our lives, has opened the door to a new world."

From *The Language of the Heart*

JANUARY 20

"I Had Lost the War!"

TORONTO, ONTARIO, NOVEMBER 1952

"A while ago a speaker said that it was no use admitting that one was an alcoholic unless the admittance was accompanied by a realization of what being an alcoholic really meant. ... He said there was no use my making the admission even in the full realization of what it meant, unless I accepted the fact that I was an alcoholic without resentment."

From *Step By Step*

JANUARY 21

"Awareness"

VIETNAM, SEPTEMBER 1974

———

"All turmoil comes from the deep,
nagging feeling that we should
be different from what we are. ... If
we could totally accept who and
what we are (changing each instant),
we would find ourselves moving
in the silent immenseness of now."

———

JANUARY 22

"Planning, Not Projection"
OCTOBER 1992

———

"As the chaotic world of the drinking alcoholic is replaced by one of stability in sobriety it becomes apparent that plans can be made to encourage positive living. For example: planning holidays, dental appointments and the household budget. We cannot plan that it will be the best holiday ever, that no dental work is required, or that our monetary fortunes will remain the same; that would be projecting. We plan plans, not results."

———

From AA Grapevine

JANUARY 23

"A Gift of Prayer"
NOVEMBER 1967

———

"I seek strength not to be superior
to my brothers, but to be able to fight
my greatest enemy—myself."

———

From *Spiritual Awakenings*

JANUARY 24

"This Matter of Fear"

AA CO-FOUNDER, BILL W., JANUARY 1962

———

"Let us always love the best in others,
and never fear their worst."

———

From *The Language of the Heart*

JANUARY 25

"The Twelve Concepts"

AA CO-FOUNDER, BILL W., PUBLISHED IN
GRAPEVINE SEPTEMBER 1990

———

"We should always realize that change does not necessarily spell progress. We are sure that each new group of workers in world service will be tempted to try all sorts of innovations that may often produce little more than a painful repetition of earlier mistakes. ... And if mistaken departures are nevertheless made, these Concepts may then provide a ready means of safe return to an operating balance that might otherwise take years of floundering to rediscover."

———

From AA Grapevine

JANUARY 26

"Not on Fire"

MESA, ARIZONA, MARCH 2010

———

"There has to be something to be grateful for if I am only willing to change my attitude and look for it."

———

JANUARY 27

"A Maze of Half-Measures"

ROCHESTER, MICHIGAN, APRIL 1986

———

"It took two years to learn that
I wasn't getting anywhere because
I was always in such a hurry."

———

From AA Grapevine

JANUARY 28

"Awareness"

VIETNAM, SEPTEMBER 1974

"Demands, hopes, yearnings, and desires tie us to the static horror and the utter futility of the forever departed past and the never-arriving future. To want nothing—to know that we cannot *make* anything happen—brings inner and outer joy, total fulfillment."

From *Spiritual Awakenings*

JANUARY 29

"I Had Lost the War!"

TORONTO, ONTARIO, NOVEMBER 1952

———

"There was no use in my wondering
why or when I became an alcoholic
for the very simple reason that it
wouldn't change my condition; even
if I did find the answer, I would still
be an alcoholic."

———

From *Step By Step*

JANUARY 30

"Tools for Life"

NEW YORK, NEW YORK, JANUARY 2006

———

"Whenever I am gripped by fear of an unknown future and all my projections are negative, I do what my sponsor directed me to do. I wriggle my toes and come back into the safety of the moment."

———

From *Beginners' Book*

JANUARY 31

"One Little Secret of a Happy Life"
NOVEMBER 1946

———

"Tomorrow is never ours until
it becomes today."

———

From Beginners' Book

FEBRUARY

FEBRUARY 1

"Mesmerized by Sanity"

LONDON, ENGLAND, FEBRUARY 1997

———

"These days I find that nothing is as precious as my sanity. I used to be addicted to drama and could only function on excitement and high levels of adrenaline. It's very different today. ... It's all very ordinary and average and sane, and I wouldn't trade it for anything."

———

From *Spiritual Awakenings*

FEBRUARY 2

"Tradition Two"

AA CO-FOUNDER, BILL W., JANUARY 1948

———

"We have, in AA, no coercive human authority. Because each AA, of necessity, has a sensitive and responsive conscience, and because alcohol will discipline him severely if he backslides, we are finding we have little need for manmade rules or regulations."

———

From *The Language of the Heart*

FEBRUARY 3

"Paradoxes of Sobriety"

KEEG O HARBOR, MICHIGAN, JUNE 1998

———

"AA has taught me that I'm
the architect of my own success or
happiness. The quality of my
sobriety is up to me—it will be
what I want it to be."

———

From *Beginners' Book*

FEBRUARY 4

"Spirituality"

ALVA, OKLAHOMA, JANUARY 1952

———

"The Twelve Steps are not steps
to take progressively in order
to arrive at a conclusion, but a code
for living—the constitution of
a way of life."

———

From AA Grapevine

FEBRUARY 5

"A Lifetime Supply"

KATHMANDU, JULY 1995

———

"If I simply let go of a character defect—release it—my Higher Power will replace it with a character asset. As I release anger, I find that I am friendlier. As I release hate, I become more loving. As I release fear, I become more secure."

———

From *Beginners' Book*

FEBRUARY 6

"AA Communication Can Cross All Boundaries"

AA CO-FOUNDER, BILL W., OCTOBER 1959

———

"Everyone must agree that we AAs are unbelievably fortunate people; fortunate that we have suffered so much; fortunate that we can know, understand and love each other so supremely well. ... Indeed most of us are well aware that these are rare gifts which have their true origin in our kinship born of a common suffering and a common deliverance by the Grace of God."

———

From *The Language of the Heart*

FEBRUARY 7

"AA's Steps Lead to—Spiritual Awakening"

HANKINS, NEW YORK, MAY 1967

―――

"I am learning, when looking for signs of spiritual awakening in myself, to look, not for bright lights or emotional upheavals ... but for sobriety, stability, responsibility, meaning, satisfaction, joy. These are the marks of the beginning of spiritual awakening."

―――

From *Spiritual Awakenings*

FEBRUARY 8

"Circles of Sobriety"

CHESTERTOWN, NEW YORK, JANUARY 2006

———

"It's important to monitor my
thinking, to be conscious of what
thoughts I'm hugging to my
heart, inviting to stay in my mind,
encouraging to hang around
my head."

———

From *Beginners' Book*

FEBRUARY 9

"Toward Reality"

NEW YORK, NEW YORK, APRIL 1980

———

"The beginning of maturing for me
was becoming willing to try to
face the realities of my own life, a day
at a time, and letting go of my
childhood fantasies of living happily
ever after in a perfect world made
up of perfect people."

———

From *Spiritual Awakenings*

FEBRUARY 10

"Patience"

NORTH HOLLYWOOD, CALIFORNIA, JUNE 1980

––––––

"Not until I became aware that God's delay is not necessarily God's denial of prayer, was I willing to let a Power greater than myself determine how and when I was to receive the things I truly needed, rather than the things for which I howled."

––––––

From *Spiritual Awakenings*

FEBRUARY 11

"Why Alcoholics Anonymous Is Anonymous"

AA CO-FOUNDER, BILL W., JANUARY 1955

———

"The temporary or seeming
good can often be the deadly enemy
of the permanent best."

———

From *The Language of the Heart*

FEBRUARY 12

"The Hoper"

PHILADELPHIA, PENNSYLVANIA, APRIL 1990

———

"Hope is tremendous progress for someone who once was 'hopeless.'"

———

From AA Grapevine

FEBRUARY 13

"How Is My Now?"

ATLANTA, GEORGIA, AUGUST 2001

———

"I borrowed others' faith for a long time, and now I'm beginning to get a bit of my own."

———

From *Beginners' Book*

FEBRUARY 14

"The Next Frontier: Emotional Sobriety"

AA CO-FOUNDER, BILL W., JANUARY 1958

"My stability came out of trying to give, not out of demanding that I receive."

From *The Language of the Heart*

FEBRUARY 15

"Tolerance Is Important"

TUSCOLA, ILLINOIS, MAY 1950

———

"Through our failures and trials we get the opportunity to soundly test our merits and virtues."

———

From AA Grapevine

FEBRUARY 16

"Stepping into the Sunlight"
LA CANADA, CALIFORNIA, NOVEMBER 1989

———

"Whereas I used to function at two speeds—fast and stopped—a daily fix of meditation averages those two extremes out to a more gentle and efficient cruise rate."

———

From *Spiritual Awakenings*

FEBRUARY 17

"The Portals of Service"

OLYMPIA, WASHINGTON, SEPTEMBER 2006

———

"Whether it was pouring coffee in my home group, or going on a Twelfth-Step call, I entered a new pattern of thinking: I thought not only about myself, but about others."

———

From *Beginners' Book*

FEBRUARY 18

"Modesty One Plank for Good Public Relations"

AA CO-FOUNDER, BILL W., AUGUST 1945

———

"We need to constantly scrutinize ourselves carefully, in order to make everlastingly certain that we shall always be strong enough and single-purposed enough from within, to relate ourselves rightly to the world without."

———

From *The Language of the Heart*

FEBRUARY 19

"Trusting the Silence"
ANONYMOUS, NOVEMBER 1991

———

"Often in sobriety, I've prayed when I needed to meditate. I've yammered at God so much that God can't get a word in edgewise. (What I practice with people, I cannot help but practice with God.) To me, meditation is simply being quiet and listening for a change. It is buttoning up my lip—and my mind that yaps even when my mouth is shut."

———

From *Beginners' Book*

FEBRUARY 20

"Okay, God ..."

HOUSTON, TEXAS, OCTOBER 1985

———

"I politely invited God to spend the day with me (like a visiting relative or friend), and instantly began a mental dialogue with God. ... I realized that in the process of introducing myself to God, I was getting a good look at who I really was."

———

From *Spiritual Awakenings*

FEBRUARY 21

"Tools for Life"

NEW YORK, JANUARY 2006

———

"Turn toward that power and ask
for help whenever you feel
disturbed or afraid, the way a plant
turns toward the light."

———

From *Beginners' Book*

FEBRUARY 22

"AA Tomorrow"

AA CO-FOUNDER, BILL W., JULY 1960

"As we better use the 'language of the heart,' our communications grow apace: already we find ourselves in safe passage through all those barriers of distance and language, of social distinction, nationality and creed, that so divide the world of our time."

From *The Language of the Heart*

FEBRUARY 23

"The Impossible Dream"

ISLAMORADA, FLORIDA, NOVEMBER 1971

———

"I am free to like and enjoy *what I have*. I don't need to exhibit my high values by hating my rowboat for not being a yacht, my house for not being a palace, my child for not being a prodigy."

———

From *The Best of the Grapevine, Volume I*

FEBRUARY 24

"Tradition Five"

AA CO-FOUNDER, BILL W., APRIL 1948

———

"May we never forget that we live by
the grace of God—on borrowed time."

———

From *The Language of the Heart*

FEBRUARY 25

"On the Beach"

LAKE WORTH, FLORIDA, APRIL 1987

———

"If I try to soar with the eagles, I'm
likely to appear more of a turkey."

———

From AA Grapevine

FEBRUARY 26

"Binge Thinker"

AMES, IOWA, JULY 2010

"Long before I was a binge drinker, I was a binge thinker. I tended to think incessantly, as if this were an essential part of staying alive. My mind either had no 'off' switch, or, if it did, I had no idea where it was."

From AA Grapevine

FEBRUARY 27

"AA's Steps Lead to—Spiritual Awakening"

HANKINS, NEW YORK, MAY 1967

———

"Spiritual awakening ... begins
with knowledge and acceptance of
the truth about ourselves."

———

From *Spiritual Awakenings*

FEBRUARY 28

"Honest, Open-Minded, Willing"
WORCESTER, MASSACHUSETTS, MARCH 1952

———

"Those of us who saw the shadow
of the butterfly net overhead
are blessed if we get to know that
an open mind can save."

———

From AA Grapevine

MARCH

MARCH 1

"Tradition Three"

AA CO-FOUNDER, BILL W., FEBRUARY 1948

———

"We believe that any two or three alcoholics gathered together for sobriety may call themselves an AA group provided that, as a group, they have no other affiliation."

———

From *The Language of the Heart*

MARCH 2

"What a Sponsor Is and Is Not"
BERLIN, CONNECTICUT, SEPTEMBER 2004

———

"Today I have a clearer perspective on what my role as a sponsor is and isn't. It is to stay sober, be available to listen, share my thoughts, pray for others, and let them live their own lives. It is not to 'fix' anyone, get them sober, make them happy, demand they conform, or make their decisions."

———

From AA Grapevine

MARCH 3

"Who Is a Member of Alcoholics Anonymous?"

AA CO-FOUNDER, BILL W., AUGUST 1946

"Two or three years ago the Central Office asked the groups to list their membership rules and send them in. After they arrived we set them all down. They took a great many sheets of paper. A little reflection upon these many rules brought us to an astonishing conclusion. If all of these edicts had been in force everywhere at once, it would have been practically impossible for any alcoholic to have ever joined Alcoholics Anonymous."

From *The Language of the Heart*

MARCH 4

"Kindred Spirits"

SAN PEDRO, CALIFORNIA, MARCH 2009

———

"I like to say that AA is a program
you can use to learn to follow the will
of your higher self."

———

From AA Grapevine

MARCH 5

"A Smile to Offer"

RALEIGH, NORTH CAROLINA, JULY 2006

———

"Today, the two most important
things in recovery for me are
willingness and action. ... Today, I
have a smile that I can offer other
alcoholics."

———

From AA Grapevine

MARCH 6

"Someone to Help"

PERRY, FLORIDA, JULY 2009

———

"AA isn't for the people who need it
or for the people who want it;
it's for the people who are willing to
do the work to get it."

———

From AA Grapevine

MARCH 7

"Who Is a Member of Alcoholics Anonymous?"

AA CO-FOUNDER, BILL W., AUGUST 1946

———

"Those who slip, those who panhandle, those who scandalize, those with mental twists, those who rebel at the program, those who trade on the AA reputation—all such persons seldom harm an AA group for long. ... They oblige us to cultivate patience, tolerance, and humility."

———

From *The Language of the Heart*

MARCH 8

"Live and Let Live"

WEST SPRINGFIELD, MASSACHUSETTS, JUNE 2002

———

"We have grown from two people
to two million. ... We must be doing
something right."

———

From AA Grapevine

MARCH 9

"Fledgling Sponsor"

MARTINSVILLE, VIRGINIA, MARCH 2009

———

"I remember asking my sponsor,
'When do I start the Steps?'
He replied, 'When do you want to
get well?'"

———

From AA Grapevine

MARCH 10

"My Good Sponsor"
ROCKY HILL, CONNECTICUT, JULY 1973

————

"Few victims of this illness can
expect sobriety without a major
change in most aspects of living."

————

From AA Grapevine

MARCH 11

"More Questions Than Answers"
DORCHESTER, MASSACHUSETTS, MARCH 1989

————

"The more I learn the more there is to learn."

————

From AA Grapevine

MARCH 12

"Live and Let Live"

WEST SPRINGFIELD, MASSACHUSETTS, JUNE 2002

———

"All of us in AA have a right to
our own opinion, even if that opinion
is that somebody else's opinion
is not as good as ours. ... The whole
structure of AA is based on a
democratic spirit. There are no
bosses or gurus."

———

From AA Grapevine

MARCH 13

"The Value of Life"

BLYTHE, CALIFORNIA, JUNE 2005

———

"When the shadows of my past
were placed in the light, I was
thankful for the 'design for living'
that the Twelve Steps provide.
It helps me to handle the shock of
who I was, who I am today, and
who I want to be."

———

From *Emotional Sobriety*

MARCH 14

"Our Critics Can Be Our Benefactors"

AA CO-FOUNDER, BILL W., APRIL 1963

———

"In the years ahead we shall, of course, make mistakes. Experience has taught us that we need have no fear of doing this, providing that we always remain willing to confess our faults and to correct them promptly."

———

From *The Language of the Heart*

MARCH 15

"Sponsorship"
LAWTON, OKLAHOMA, FEBRUARY 1955

———

"It is very possible that I might not be the most suitable person to sponsor a particular new member. I might be unsuited by my personality, by my education (or lack of education) or by my profession. For the same reasons I might be just the one to sponsor someone else."

———

From AA Grapevine

MARCH 16

"Growth"

HOUSTON, TEXAS, JUNE 1976

"It seems to me that I achieve
growth by leaving things out—when
I don't say the cross word, when
I don't answer sarcastically. If I can
delay only one second, maybe
two, I have time to ask myself, 'Do
I really want to say that?'"

From *Emotional Sobriety*

MARCH 17

"Spiritual Coffee-Making"

VINTON, IOWA, AUGUST 2001

———

"I need my home group to be a place where I can learn to practice the principles embodied in the Twelve Steps with other alcoholics. This sets in motion my willingness to practice these principles in all my affairs, including my home life."

———

From *Emotional Sobriety*

MARCH 18

"Seeking Through Meditation"
NEW YORK, NEW YORK, APRIL 1969

———

"The mind will often drift away into daydreams, but patiently we turn our attention back to the truth and the reality of existence and experience, all as it is happening right now."

———

MARCH 19

"In All Our Affairs"

WESTPORT, CONNECTICUT, JULY 1956

———

"My belief in a Higher Power is as strong as it was when I went to my first AA meeting and accepted the first and second Steps as simply and as trustfully as a child accepts its mother's milk. ... So what on earth was I looking for? I just don't know. I guess I wanted a little Tinker Bell all my own to show me the right and only way out of every situation."

———

From Emotional Sobriety

MARCH 20

"Beyond My Reach"

LANSING, MICHIGAN, MAY 2009

———

"When it seems like love just isn't
enough, I remind myself that
it is all I have to give beyond my
experience, strength and hope."

———

From AA Grapevine

MARCH 21

"Win Or Lose"

ESCONDIDO, CALIFORNIA, AUGUST 2001

———

"Success and failure share a common denominator. ... Both are temporary."

———

From *Emotional Sobriety*

MARCH 22

"God As We Understand Him: The Dilemma of No Faith"

AA CO-FOUNDER, BILL W., APRIL 1961

————

"Faith is more than our greatest gift; its sharing with others is our greatest responsibility."

————

From *The Language of the Heart*

MARCH 23

"Humility for Today"
AA CO-FOUNDER, BILL W., JUNE 1961

———

"Excessive guilt or rebellion leads
to spiritual poverty."

———

From *The Language of the Heart*

MARCH 24

"Winners and Whiners"

PORT TOWNSEND, WASHINGTON,
OCTOBER 1994

———

"There are winners and whiners,
and sometimes I seem to
embody both. I am, as my friends
remind me, a human being."

———

From *Emotional Sobriety*

MARCH 25

"'Rules' Dangerous but Unity Vital"
AA CO-FOUNDER, BILL W., SEPTEMBER 1945

"During his first AA years every AA has had plenty of the urge to revolt against authority. I know I did, and can't claim to be over it yet. I've also served my time as a maker of rules, a regulator of other people's conduct. ... I can now look back upon such experiences with much amusement. And gratitude as well."

From *The Language of the Heart*

MARCH 26

"Is 'Agnostic' a Nasty Word?"

CASPER, WYOMING, SEPTEMBER 1969

———

"Spiritual growth and experiences are not limited to orthodox believers in a deity, any more than the disease of alcoholism is limited to skid-row bums."

———

From AA Grapevine

MARCH 27

"Growth"

HOUSTON, TEXAS, JUNE 1976

———

"I have discovered a new way to learn—by shutting my mouth and listening. ... It's not so much what I'm doing as what I'm not doing. I'm not talking. So I'm open; I'm teachable."

———

From Emotional Sobriety

MARCH 28

"How Is My Now?"

ATLANTA, GEORGIA, AUGUST 2001

―――――

"I was so busy juggling the regrets of the past with the expectations of tomorrow I had no time for living in the present."

―――――

From *Beginners' Book*

MARCH 29

"Modesty One Plank for Good Public Relations"

AA CO-FOUNDER, BILL W., AUGUST 1945

———

"Personal glorification, overweening pride, consuming ambition, exhibitionism, intolerant smugness, money or power madness, refusal to admit mistakes and learn from them, self-satisfaction, lazy complacency— these and many more are the garden variety of ills which so often beset movements as well as individuals."

———

From *The Language of the Heart*

MARCH 30

"'Rules' Dangerous but Unity Vital"

AA CO-FOUNDER, BILL W., SEPTEMBER 1945

———

"It is out of our discussions, our differences of opinion, our daily experiences, and our general consent that the true answers must finally come."

———

From *The Language of the Heart*

MARCH 31

"Breaking Through Ritual"

ORCHARD LAKE, MICHIGAN, DECEMBER 1966

———

"Only a gift given in love and gratitude is blessed to the giver and precious to the receiver."

———

From *Step By Step*

APRIL

APRIL 1

"The Individual in Relation to AA as a Group"

AA CO-FOUNDER, BILL W., JULY 1946

———

"In the life of each AA member, there still lurks a tyrant. His name is alcohol."

———

From *The Language of the Heart*

APRIL 2

"Winners and Whiners"

PORT TOWNSEND, WASHINGTON,
OCTOBER 1994

———

"What I've had to figure out is that
I can't figure anything out."

———

From Emotional Sobriety

APRIL 3

"A New Way of Looking at Life"

COLUMBUS, OHIO, APRIL 1981

———

"My life and the lives of those around me do, in fact, form their own parts in a symphony of interaction."

———

From *Voices of Long-Term Sobriety*

APRIL 4

"God As We Understand Him: The Dilemma of No Faith"

AA CO-FOUNDER, BILL W., APRIL 1961

———

"The phrase 'God as we understand him' is perhaps the most important expression to be found in our whole AA vocabulary. Within the compass of these five significant words there can be included every kind and degree of faith, together with the positive assurance that each of us may choose his own."

———

From *The Language of the Heart*

APRIL 5

"Reciprocal Strength"
VANCOUVER, BRITISH COLUMBIA, JANUARY 1998

———

"I've likened that transforming
instant, when despair gave way
to a glimmer of hope, to a tiny flower
sprung into bloom amid the
bombed-out wreckage of my life.
Thanks to AA, that tiny
bloom was to become a garden."

———

From *Voices of Long-Term Sobriety*

APRIL 6

"It Takes What It Takes"

POMPANO BEACH, FLORIDA, JUNE 1978

———

"Sobriety does interesting things to
the mind—clears it up some, lets
a bit of honesty and truth filter in,
and begins to demand reality."

———

From *Step By Step*

APRIL 7

"Mirror, Mirror, On the Wall"

RENTON, WASHINGTON, OCTOBER 1987

———

"Sometimes taking somebody else's inventory can be most beneficial. When I was doing my Fourth Step, an old-timer suggested I list the names of those against whom I held resentments, followed by two or three sentences describing what they had done to earn my displeasure. Then, after putting the list aside for a day, I was to cross off each person's name and replace it with my own."

———

From *Step By Step*

APRIL 8

"The Individual in Relation to AA as a Group"

AA CO-FOUNDER, BILL W., JULY 1946

———

"So long as there is the slightest interest in sobriety, the most unmoral, the most antisocial, the most critical alcoholic may gather about him a few kindred spirits and announce to us that a new Alcoholics Anonymous group has been formed. Anti-God, anti-medicine, anti-our recovery program, even anti-each other—these rampant individuals are still an AA group if *they think so!*"

———

From *The Language of the Heart*

APRIL 9

"Garden Hose Sobriety"

EL PASO, TEXAS, OCTOBER 2006

———

"When I go to a meeting today, I no longer have the delusion that I am supporting a good cause. I need AA; AA did quite well without me during my ten years of self-exile. I go to AA meetings today to hear and see how God is working. When I share at a meeting, it is not to try and 'help' those poor wretches, it is because I need their help and guidance."

———

From *Voices of Long-Term Sobriety*

APRIL 10

"Why I Keep Coming Back"

TOLEDO, OHIO, MAY 2001

———

"AA is a caring community ...
of people who understand how
others can be trapped in
deep loneliness and despair."

———

From *Voices of Long-Term Sobriety*

APRIL 11

"The Real Thing"

NEW YORK, NEW YORK, FEBRUARY 2001

———

"An old-timer once told me that he believed that AA was a great leveler: When you're up high, your friends help bring you down a little bit. When you're down low, they help bring you up a little bit."

———

From *Voices of Long-Term Sobriety*

APRIL 12

"From Rags to Riches"

CORNWALL, ONTARIO, JANUARY 2005

———

"My soul remained a mystery until my Higher Power settled inside me, appearing to me as a very real feeling of love and caring. Kindness slowly took precedence, and I became comfortable with the idea that I didn't need a drink."

———

From *Voices of Long-Term Sobriety*

APRIL 13

"Tradition Four"

AA CO-FOUNDER, BILL W., MARCH 1948

———

"Those severe growing pains which invariably follow any radical departure from AA Tradition can be absolutely relied upon to bring an erring group back into line. An AA group need not be coerced by any human government over and above its own members. Their own experience, plus AA opinion in surrounding groups, plus God's prompting in their group conscience would be sufficient."

———

From *The Language of the Heart*

APRIL 14

"A Means to a Beginning"
GRAND ISLAND, NEBRASKA, FEBRUARY 1984

"Sponsorship is a bridge to trusting the human race, the very race we once resigned from. In learning to trust, we are strengthening our sobriety."

From AA Grapevine

APRIL 15

"Win Or Lose"

ESCONDIDO, CALIFORNIA, AUGUST 2001

———

"My sponsor ... gave me some good advice. 'Take the words *success* and *failure* out of your vocabulary. Replace them with *honesty* and *effort*.'"

———

From *Emotional Sobriety*

APRIL 16

"An English Gentleman"

CLEVEDON, SOMERSET, ENGLAND
DECEMBER 1999

———

"I make a conscious effort to
keep it simple, because the simpler
I make it, the happier I become."

———

From *Voices of Long-Term Sobriety*

APRIL 17

"The Real Thing"

NEW YORK, NEW YORK, FEBRUARY 2001

———

"As an individual I am so small I'm almost totally meaningless in the universe; it's almost as if I didn't exist. But not quite. ... As small as I am, I'm not totally meaningless."

———

From *Voices of Long-Term Sobriety*

APRIL 18

"Why Alcoholics Anonymous Is Anonymous"

AA CO-FOUNDER, BILL W., JANUARY 1955

———

"We found that each of us had to make willing sacrifices ... for the common welfare."

———

From *The Language of the Heart*

APRIL 19

"Absolutely Richard"

SANTA CRUZ, CALIFORNIA, APRIL 1998

———

"The spirit of AA has been with me ...
for better or for worse, for richer or
for poorer, in sickness and in health."

———

APRIL 20

"This Matter of Honesty"

AA CO-FOUNDER, BILL W., AUGUST 1961

———

"The deception of others is
nearly always rooted in the deception
of ourselves."

———

From *The Language of the Heart*

APRIL 21

"Truth"

KEY WEST, FLORIDA, AUGUST 1973

———

"Truth is to inner space what
sunshine is to a garden."

———

APRIL 22

"From Make-Believe to Belief"

CHARLESTON, WEST VIRGINIA, JUNE 1981

———

"I was relieved to learn that I didn't have to believe, only be willing to believe. This I could do."

———

From *Voices of Long-Term Sobriety*

APRIL 23

"Seasons of Real Joy"

AA CO-FOUNDER, BILL W., REPRINTED JULY 1993

———

"Some people think God made life just for happiness, but I find myself unable to share that view. I think he made life for growth and that he permits pain as the touchstone of it all. Happiness—at the very least, satisfaction—is a byproduct of really trying to grow. And seasons of real joy are but the occasional byproducts of the process. Which, in eternity, will be the eventual fulfillment. Meantime, we seem to be pilgrims on a road—one which you and I are completely confident leads into the arms of God."

———

From AA Grapevine

APRIL 24

"Centrifugal Force"

NEW YORK, NEW YORK, APRIL 2004

———

"I need to constantly inch forward
in AA, closer to the center, to
avoid being thrown from the spinning
wheel that is my life."

———

APRIL 25

"More Will Be Revealed"

PORTLAND, OREGON, OCTOBER 1998

————

"I was attracted to AA because it
excluded no one, and I am grateful
for the lessons I've learned
over the years: that we stop fighting
anyone or anything; that it is
the details of what I do that make me
who I am; that my perception of
life is ever-changing and evolving;
that the basic 'suggestions' I
heard when I entered the Fellowship
have been a continuous part
of my life; that as long as I stay
an active member of AA, more
will be revealed."

————

From *Voices of Long-Term Sobriety*

APRIL 26

"Leadership in AA: Ever a Vital Need"

AA CO-FOUNDER, BILL W., APRIL 1959

———

"There are always the constructive critics, our friends indeed. We should never fail to give them a careful hearing."

———

From *The Language of the Heart*

APRIL 27

"From Rags to Riches"

CORNWALL, ONTARIO, JANUARY 2005

———

"Serenity and peace of mind are a
direct result of accepting our
lives as they are at this moment, and
all the money in the world
cannot purchase this kind of peace."

———

From *Voices of Long-Term Sobriety*

APRIL 28

"The Next Frontier: Emotional Sobriety"

AA CO-FOUNDER, BILL W., JANUARY 1958

———

"I could not avail myself of God's love until I was able to offer it back to him by loving others as he would have me. And I couldn't possibly do that so long as I was victimized by false dependencies."

———

From *The Language of the Heart*

APRIL 29

"Taking the Time to Listen"

JACKSONVILLE BEACH, FLORIDA, DECEMBER 1997

———

"When I look into the eyes of the
person next to me and ask, 'How are
you?', I will take the time to listen.
I want to keep in mind that at any
given time, each of us may need
the same love and support as someone
who is attending their first meeting."

———

From *Voices of Long-Term Sobriety*

APRIL 30

"Why I Keep Coming Back"

TOLEDO, OHIO, MAY 2001

———

"Every recovery, though it may
go unnoticed, improves the world
in some way."

———

MAY

MAY 1

"Finding Self-Forgiveness"
MEMPHIS, TENNESSEE, OCTOBER 1977

———

"The actual experience of turning myself inside out for the first time in the presence of an AA member left me drained and numb; but when feeling started to come back, I found that I had changed. For the first time in my AA experience, I could feel the sunshine of God's love on my wounds, and true peace of mind."

———

From *Step By Step*

MAY 2

"A 5,000-Mile Discussion"

SECUNDERABAD, INDIA, DECEMBER 1982

———

"I cannot adequately describe how
light I feel since I took the Fifth Step,
and how soundly I sleep."

———

From *Step By Step*

MAY 3

"H-E-L-P"

PHOENIX, ARIZONA, APRIL 2011

———

"The rewards of asking for help—
increased humility, connection, and
trust—are well worth the effort."

———

From AA Grapevine

MAY 4

"Tradition Five"

AA CO-FOUNDER, BILL W., APRIL 1948

———

"We shall never be at our best except when we hew only to the primary spiritual aim of AA. That of carrying its message to the alcoholic who still suffers alcoholism."

———

From *The Language of the Heart*

MAY 5

"Freedom Began in Prison"
UNIVERSAL CITY, CALIFORNIA, FEBRUARY 1970

———

"Good things increase in
direct proportion to my willingness
to become teachable."

———

From AA Grapevine

MAY 6

"The Guidance of AA's World Affairs"

AA CO-FOUNDER, BILL W., JANUARY 1966

———

"All AA progress can be reckoned in terms of just two words: humility and responsibility."

———

From *The Language of the Heart*

MAY 7

"A United Message of Recovery"
DECATUR, GEORGIA, MAY 1994

———

"It is our experience as alcoholics
that makes us of unique
value. ... We can approach sufferers
as no one else can."

———

From AA Grapevine

MAY 8

"Freedom Under God: The Choice Is Ours"

AA CO-FOUNDER, BILL W., NOVEMBER 1960

———

"Only mutual trust can be the foundation for great love—each of us for the other, and all of us for God."

———

From *The Language of the Heart*

MAY 9

"Why Have a Home Group?"
NEOSHO, MISSOURI, SEPTEMBER 1986

———

"It's not the wonderful people I've met from throughout these great lands who have helped keep me sober most of the time, but those wonderful people sitting around the table in my hometown who loved me when I could not love, who waited for me to quit lying, who tolerated me when I would be part of nothing, and who never asked me to leave when I was obnoxious. Because of their love and patience, I was able to get outside of myself and make some sort of commitment to the group."

———

From *The Home Group*

MAY 10

"Right Here Right Now!"

SANTA BARBARA, CALIFORNIA, SEPTEMBER 1960

———

"Tomorrow—and all the tomorrows to come—are but extensions of right here, right now."

———

From AA Grapevine and *A.A. in Prison:*
Inmate to Inmate

MAY 11

"Why Can't We Join AA, Too?"

AA CO-FOUNDER, BILL W., OCTOBER 1947

———

"We are alcoholics. Even though now recovered, we are never too far removed from the possibility of fresh personal disaster. Each knows he must observe a high degree of honesty, humility, and tolerance, or else drink again."

———

From *The Language of the Heart*

MAY 12

"Learning to Handle Sobriety"
CONNECTICUT, MARCH 1975

———

"We reject fantasizing and accept reality. And we find it beautiful. For, at last, we are at peace with ourselves. And with others. And with God."

———

MAY 13

"8-½"

BOWLING GREEN, KENTUCKY, OCTOBER 1986

———

"When I can identify my own short-comings in another, the battleground between us is removed."

———

MAY 14

"If You Can't Live or Die, Make Coffee!"

FREEPORT, NEW YORK, SEPTEMBER 1988

———

"Why dwell on what you can't do? ...
Why not concentrate on what you *can*
do and do it?"

———

From *The Home Group*

MAY 15

"Comments on Wylie Ideas"
DR. HARRY TIEBOUT, SEPTEMBER 1944

———

"A religious, or spiritual experience,
is the act of giving up reliance on one's
own omnipotence."

———

From *The Language of the Heart*

MAY 16

"A Long Way From Home"

MORATUWA, SRI LANKA, SEPTEMBER 1994

———

"I was told when I got sober that I could act my way into right thinking, but I could never think my way into right action."

———

From *AA Around the World*

MAY 17

"Know Thyself!"

POUGHKEEPSIE, NEW YORK, JULY 2011

———

"I need to remember how humiliated, confused, insecure and frightened I felt at my first meeting, and compare that to how I feel today."

———

From AA Grapevine

MAY 18

"Just Keep On Going"

NEW CANAAN, CONNECTICUT, APRIL 1976

———

"Trying to figure it all out in my head brings on waves of fear, anxiety, and self-reproach. So I say, 'What can I do for myself and others today?'"

———

MAY 19

"Citizens of the World"

AA CO-FOUNDER, BILL W., AS QUOTED IN
JUNE 1975

———

"In AA we aim not only for sobriety—
we try again to become citizens of
the world that we rejected, and of the
world that once rejected us."

———

MAY 20

"People and Principles"
JACKSON, MICHIGAN, OCTOBER 1971

———

"Human beings come and go, but
principles go on and on."

———

MAY 21

"Short Takes"

BINGHAMTON, NEW YORK, JULY 1967

———

"I build today the road I travel tomorrow."

———

From AA Grapevine

MAY 22

"Bright Promise"

ATLANTA, GEORGIA, JULY 1956

"The most difficult thing a man
can do is turn his eyes inward upon
his real self."

From AA Grapevine and *A.A. in Prison:*
Inmate to Inmate

MAY 23

"A Bigger God"

LOS ANGELES, CALIFORNIA, MARCH 2002

———

"When I'm in fear, my sponsor always tells me, 'Maybe you should get a bigger God.'"

———

From *Beginners' Book*

MAY 24

"We Came of Age"

AA CO-FOUNDER, BILL W., SEPTEMBER 1950

––––––

"Simplicity, devotion, steadfastness,
and loyalty; these, we remembered,
were the hallmarks of character
which Dr. Bob had well implanted in
so many of us."

––––––

From *The Language of the Heart*

MAY 25

"Those Depressions—Make Them Work for Good!"

NEW YORK, NEW YORK, AUGUST 1948

———

"We will still have daydreams. ...
But they will be constructive dreams,
rather than mere flights of fancy."

———

MAY 26

"Love"

NORTH HOLLYWOOD, CALIFORNIA,
SEPTEMBER 1988

———

"When we concentrate on loving those we think are unlovable, we find out how expansive love is."

———

MAY 27

"A Way of Life"
CHICAGO, ILLINOIS, JULY 1946

———

"In the Twelve Steps, AA offers not
a theory, not a hypothesis, not a pious
hope, not—thank God—wistful
or wishful thinking, but an historical
record of how more than 25,000
[now over 2,000,000] alcoholics
achieved sobriety."

———

MAY 28

"Responsibility Is the Name of the Game"

VAN NUYS, CALIFORNIA, NOVEMBER 1966

———

"I am responsible for reporting for duty and making the effort to overcome the adversity, and in so doing to overcome myself."

———

MAY 29

"Tradition Five:
What a Group 'Ought' to Be"

MAY 2006

———

"Whatever strengthens the spirituality of the group strengthens my spirituality, and vice versa."

———

From AA Grapevine

MAY 30

"The Physicians"

AA CO-FOUNDER, BILL W., AUGUST 1957

———

"Truly transforming spiritual
experiences are nearly always
founded on calamity and collapse."

———

From *The Language of the Heart*

MAY 31

"You Call This Unity!"

PISCATAWAY, NEW JERSEY, JANUARY 1992

———

"I pray that I may continue to grow
in unselfishness, enough to
care about the lives of all alcoholics,
wherever they may be—those
that are with us and those yet to come."

———

JUNE

JUNE 1

"This Matter of Fear"

AA CO-FOUNDER, BILL W., JANUARY 1962

———

"Before the coming of faith I had lived as an alien in a cosmos that too often seemed both hostile and cruel."

———

JUNE 2

"A Whole New Outlook on Life"

DAR ES SALAAM, TANZANIA, DECEMBER 1978

———

"Not all of the problems created during the days when I hid in the fog of booze have straightened out, but I now have enough courage to face them squarely."

———

From *AA Around the World*

JUNE 3

"Services Make AA Tick"

AA CO-FOUNDER, BILL W., NOVEMBER 1951

———

"A coffeepot simmers on the kitchen stove, a hospital sobers the stricken sufferer, general headquarters broadcasts the AA message. ... All these symbolize AA in action. For action is the magic word of Alcoholics Anonymous."

———

From The Best of the Grapevine, Volume I

JUNE 4

"On Cultivating Tolerance"

AA CO-FOUNDER, DR. BOB, JULY 1944

———

"Those who follow the
AA program with the greatest
earnestness and zeal not
only maintain sobriety but
often acquire finer
characteristics and attitudes as
well. One of these is tolerance."

———

JUNE 5

"A Sense of Wonder"

SEATTLE, WASHINGTON, JUNE 1968

———

"The things that used to keep me awake nights now no longer bother me, because I can put them against the backdrop of eternity. The long, lonely winter that was alcoholism has turned into spring—the rebirth, the renewal of my life."

———

From *Spiritual Awakenings*

JUNE 6

"Love"

FAIRFIELD, CONNECTICUT, MARCH 1980

———

"I don't stand around on street corners just loving everybody today. But in an AA meeting or any AA gathering, I know I am in the kind of community of love that every therapy, religion, and philosophy desperately seeks. Love is our glue."

———

From *Spiritual Awakenings*

JUNE 7

"Sixth Step"

NEW YORK, NEW YORK, SEPTEMBER 1970

———

"I can now admit that most
of my troubles stem from
one large and glaring defect:
self-centeredness."

———

From *The Best of the Grapevine, Volume II*

JUNE 8

"Letters to the Editor"

TAMPA, FLORIDA, MAY 1945

———

"A good question to ask myself
frequently is: What am I looking for—
advice or approval?"

———

From *Thank You for Sharing*

JUNE 9

"The Invisible Line"

REDWOOD CITY, CALIFORNIA, APRIL 1993

———

"We in AA talk about crossing the invisible line into our alcoholism. What about crossing the invisible line into the program of Alcoholics Anonymous?"

———

From *Thank You for Sharing*

JUNE 10 (FOUNDERS' DAY)

"Dr. Bob—AA's Co-Founder To Be"

AA CO-FOUNDER, BILL W., JUNE 1965

———

"I knew I needed the alcoholic as much as he needed me. ... And this mutual give-and-take is at the very heart of all of AA's Twelfth Step work today. This was how to carry the message. The final missing link was located right there in my first talk with Dr. Bob."

———

From AA Grapevine

JUNE 11

"Making Room to Grow Up"
CANAAN, CONNECTICUT, JUNE 1997

———

"Instead of looking backward into the dreariness of my past, I'm looking forward to a bright future because I've finally taken responsibility for my life."

———

From *Step By Step*

JUNE 12

"Surrender—Not Self-Improvement"

ATLANTA, GEORGIA, FEBRUARY 1990

"Not to change is not to adapt; not to adapt is to become extinct."

JUNE 13

"What Is Acceptance?"

AA CO-FOUNDER, BILL W., MARCH 1962

———

"Our very first problem is to accept our present circumstances as they are, ourselves as we are, and the people about us as they are. This is to adopt a realistic humility without which no genuine advance can even begin."

———

From *The Best of the Grapevine, Volume I*

JUNE 14

"Freedom Under God: The Choice Is Ours"

AA CO-FOUNDER, BILL W., NOVEMBER 1960

"We must never be blindsided by the futile philosophy that we are just the hapless victims of our inheritance, our life experience, and our surroundings—that these are the sole forces that make our decisions for us. ... We have to believe that we can really choose."

From *The Language of the Heart*

JUNE 15

"Letting the Spirit Join In"
BUFFALO, NEW YORK, NOVEMBER 1995

———

"I no longer view the dishes as an unpleasant task. I see them as an opportunity to meditate. ... I concentrate on washing the dishes and not on what I'm going to do next. The most important thing is what's in front of me—now."

———

From *Spiritual Awakenings*

JUNE 16

"Guardian of AA: Our General Service Conference"

AA CO-FOUNDER, BILL W., APRIL 1958

"The history of AA shows that whenever a great need arises, that need is always met. In this respect, I'm quite sure that our history will go on repeating itself."

JUNE 17

"Twelve Suggested Points for AA Tradition"

AA CO-FOUNDER, BILL W., APRIL 1946

"Since personal calamity holds us in bondage no more, our most challenging concern has become the future of Alcoholics Anonymous; how to preserve among us AAs such a powerful unity that neither weakness of persons nor the strain and strife of these troubled times can harm our common cause."

From *The Language of the Heart*

JUNE 18

"Responsibility (Noun): The Ability to Respond"

BRONX, NEW YORK, SEPTEMBER 1983

"Responsibility is a gift; and although we are not obliged to receive it, we will never come to know the peace, assurance, and love of a vital sobriety until we do."

From *I Am Responsible*

JUNE 19

"The Most Beautiful Word in the English Language"

LOMBARD, ILLINOIS, FEBRUARY 1995

———

"Not drinking is the first requirement for joy; the second requirement is gratitude."

———

From *In Our Own Words*

JUNE 20

"Compassion"

GATES MILLS, OHIO, SEPTEMBER 1975

———

"Only in giving do we receive
in full measure."

———

From AA Grapevine

JUNE 21

"My Name Is Helen"

FLORIDA, JULY 1977

———

"I have begun to trust my friends
enough to lean on them."

———

JUNE 22

"Truth"

KEY WEST, FLORIDA, AUGUST 1973

———

"The world of truth is the world of what is. It is the room I sit in, the sleeping kitten, the job that must be done. It is here. It is now."

———

From AA Grapevine

JUNE 23

"The Next Frontier: Emotional Sobriety"

AA CO-FOUNDER, BILL W., JANUARY 1958

———

"Emotional and instinctual satisfactions, I saw, were really the extra dividends of having love, offering love, and expressing love appropriate to each relation of life."

———

From *The Language of the Heart*

JUNE 24

"Not On Fire"

MESA, ARIZONA, MARCH 2010

———

"No matter what is going on
in my life, no matter how
bad things seem, I can always find
something to be grateful
for if I just look hard enough."

———

From *Emotional Sobriety II*

JUNE 25

"Ten Minutes of Oneness"

SAN MATEO, CALIFORNIA, DECEMBER 1995

———

"I'm not here to change Alcoholics
Anonymous; Alcoholics Anonymous
is here to change me."

———

From *In Our Own Words*

JUNE 26

"Keeping Recovery Alive"

RALEIGH, NORTH CAROLINA, JANUARY 2000

———

"If we follow our Traditions, we will survive and, I hope, grow. The Traditions tell us to serve—not govern; to attract—not promote; to carry the message—not force it on anyone; to keep the three legacies alive: recovery, unity, and service. These are our lifelines."

———

From *I Am Responsible*

JUNE 27

"Why Alcoholics Anonymous Is Anonymous"

AA CO-FOUNDER, BILL W., JANUARY 1955

———

"Last summer I visited the Akron cemetery where Bob and Anne lie. Their simple stone says never a word about Alcoholics Anonymous. This made me so glad I cried."

———

From *The Best of the Grapevine, Volume I*

JUNE 28

"The Deeper Dimension"

DENVER, COLORADO, SEPTEMBER 1993

———

"We are all important, but not for the reasons we think."

———

From AA Grapevine

JUNE 29

"The Only Revolution"
APRIL 1976

———

"Sanity begins with the admission
of reality into the mind."

———

From AA Grapevine

JUNE 30

"The Power of Good"

PASADENA, CALIFORNIA, APRIL 1978

———

"I am trying to do what I can
to love, today. Can anything else
be more important?"

———

From Spiritual Awakenings

JULY

JULY 1

"This Matter of Fear"

AA CO-FOUNDER, BILL W., JANUARY 1962

———

"The foundation stone of freedom
from fear is that of faith:
a faith that, despite all worldly
appearances to the contrary,
causes me to believe that I live in
a universe that makes sense."

———

From *The Best of Bill*

JULY 2

"A New Truth"

LOS ANGELES, CALIFORNIA, MAY 1966

———

"AA is not a place; it's an attitude of mind, a warmth of the heart—a spiritual fourth dimension where material things can't get the upper hand."

———

From *Thank You for Sharing*

JULY 3

"Savoring Our Sobriety"
NORTH HOLLYWOOD, CALIFORNIA, AUGUST 1982

———

"At some point in each today,
we recovering alcoholics need to pay
ourselves a friendly visit."

———

JULY 4

"Another Human Being"

OCEANSIDE, NEW YORK, MAY 2012

———

"I was told when I began my own journey through the Twelve Steps that I could find God in a most unlikely place: standing smack in the middle of the truth about myself."

———

From AA Grapevine

JULY 5

"The Scariest Thing"
CARLSBAD, CALIFORNIA, JUNE 2006

———

"The group I joined saved my life. ...
For an hour, I was safe. For an
hour, I had a haven among those
whose fear had once been as
great as my own. I did not give my
fear away—they took it. They
eased it from my grasp with hugs and
laughter, with shared experience."

———

From *Emotional Sobriety*

JULY 6

"Seventh Step"

BRIGHTON, COLORADO, NOVEMBER 1970

———

"My willingness to have my defects of character removed was bolstered by the realization that little, if any, spiritual growth was possible as long as I held on to my old ideas and defects."

———

From *The Best of the Grapevine, Volume II*

JULY 7

"Winners and Whiners"

PORT TOWNSEND, WASHINGTON,
OCTOBER 1994

———

"When life is easy, I usually assume
it's God's way and I'm quite
spiritual. But when I'm in emotional
trouble, I assume life's a
drag and that God's gone fishing."

———

From *Emotional Sobriety*

JULY 8

"Truth"

KEY WEST, FLORIDA, AUGUST 1973

———

"The effort to escape from truth is the father of anxiety."

———

JULY 9

"What Is Acceptance?"

AA CO-FOUNDER, BILL W., MARCH 1962

———

"We neither ran nor fought. But accept we did. And then we began to be free."

———

From *The Language of the Heart*

JULY 10

"Don't Put It Off"

ST. PAUL, MINNESOTA, OCTOBER 1952

"I believe that a man's value to himself is the sum total of his positive reaction to the little things in life."

From *Thank You for Sharing*

JULY 11

"This Matter of Fear"

AA CO-FOUNDER, BILL W., JANUARY 1962

———

"As faith grows, so does
inner security."

———

From *The Best of Bill*

JULY 12

"This Matter of Honesty"

AA CO-FOUNDER, BILL W., AUGUST 1961

"Truth ... cut the shackles that
once bound us to alcohol. It
continues to release us from conflicts
and miseries beyond reckoning;
it banishes fear and isolation."

From *The Best of Bill*

JULY 13

"Are We Really Willing to Change?"

NEW YORK, NEW YORK, DECEMBER 1980

———

"Facing ourselves ... is often
more difficult than being honest with
another person."

———

From *Step By Step*

JULY 14

"This Matter of Honesty"
AA CO-FOUNDER, BILL W., AUGUST 1961

———

"Just how and when we tell the
truth—or keep silent—can
often reveal the difference between
genuine integrity and none at all."

———

From *The Best of Bill*

JULY 15

"Wrinkles in My Ego"

ROCHESTER, NEW YORK, OCTOBER 1979

———

"It is very difficult to steer a parked car and make much progress toward any destination. ... In short, I had to be going somewhere before I could be guided."

———

From *Step By Step*

JULY 16

"The Value of Life"

BLYTHE, CALIFORNIA, JUNE 2005

———

"I found that the little things I took for granted on a daily basis were the things that meant the most."

———

JULY 17

"A Remarkable Sensation"

THOMPSON, PENNSYLVANIA, MARCH 1997

———

"Following a spiritual path has become increasingly essential to me. Contrary to my fear that taking Step Three would condemn me to a life of brave self-sacrifice, I find instead that it frees me to think and act as my truest self."

———

From *Emotional Sobriety*

JULY 18

"The Individual in Relation to AA as a Group"

AA CO-FOUNDER, BILL W., JULY 1946

———

"I had been living too much alone, too much aloof from my fellows, and too deaf to that voice within."

———

JULY 19

"Enjoying Anonymity"
SEATTLE, WASHINGTON, JANUARY 1992

———

"Humility is a personal achievement, it cannot be given away. It comes in glimmers and grows like an ice crystal. It is fragile, too, thus requiring constant care and protection."

———

From *The Home Group*

JULY 20

"The Greatest Gift of All"

AA CO-FOUNDER, BILL W., DECEMBER 1957

———

"Regardless of worldly success or failure, regardless of pain or joy, regardless of sickness or health or even of death itself, a new life of endless possibilities can be lived if we are willing to continue our awakening, through the practice of AA's Twelve Steps."

———

From *The Language of the Heart*

JULY 21

"The Steps Are the Program"
RIVERSIDE, ILLINOIS, JULY 1975

———

"There is no you or me or them.
Everything is connected and
the salvation of each of us is linked
to the salvation of all of us."

———

JULY 22

"The Fundamentals in Retrospect"
AA CO-FOUNDER, DR. BOB, SEPTEMBER 1948

———

"We have all known and seen miracles—the healing of broken individuals, the rebuilding of broken homes. And always, it has been constructive, personal Twelfth Step work based on an ever-upward-looking faith which has done the job."

———

From *Spiritual Awakenings*

JULY 23

"Meetings in the Bank"

NEW YORK, NEW YORK, JUNE 2009

———

"The only thing that could chase
my disease was the sun rising
on a new morning. Just like when
I was counting days, and I would
wake up and think, Hey, I made it."

———

From *Emotional Sobriety II*

JULY 24

"Responsibility Is Our Theme"

AA CO-FOUNDER, BILL W., JULY 1965

———

"The essence of all growth is a
willingness to change for
the better and then an unremitting
willingness to shoulder
whatever responsibility this entails."

———

From *The Language of the Heart*

JULY 25

"Recovery Is a Wonderland"

BROOKLYN, NEW YORK, JULY 2010

———

"I've learned that I am not responsible for anyone's happiness except my own. Most importantly, I learned that true happiness is an inside job."

———

From *Emotional Sobriety II*

JULY 26

"The Faith to Believe in What Is"

KEY WEST, FLORIDA, JULY 1972

———

"The leap of faith must be taken
again and again over greater and
greater distances."

———

From AA Grapevine

JULY 27

"This Matter of Honesty"

AA CO-FOUNDER, BILL W., AUGUST 1961

———

"Had I not been blessed with wise and loving advisers, I might have cracked up long ago."

———

From *The Best of Bill*

JULY 28

"Something Revolutionary"

NAIROBI, KENYA, APRIL 1998

———

"AA may or may not get me to heaven,
but it surely got me out of hell."

———

JULY 29

"Growth"

HOUSTON, TEXAS, JUNE 1976

———

"I'm usually about eighty percent of
the problem—well, maybe sixty
percent, but the major part, you can
bet on that. If I can leave out the
largest percent (me), there is hardly
any problem at all!"

———

From *Emotional Sobriety*

JULY 30

"AA's Steps Lead to—Spiritual Awakening"

HANKINS, NEW YORK, MAY 1967

———

"The experience of reality does not have to be postponed."

———

From *Spiritual Awakenings*

JULY 31

"Savoring Our Sobriety"
NORTH HOLLYWOOD, CALIFORNIA, AUGUST 1982

———

"Because each of us, at any moment, is the sum total of every choice he or she has ever made, it is not sheer fantasy to expect each day to be the very best day we have yet lived."

———

From *Emotional Sobriety*

AUGUST

AUGUST 1

"The Next Frontier: Emotional Sobriety"

AA CO-FOUNDER, BILL W., JANUARY 1958

———

"If we examine every disturbance we have, great or small, we will find at the root of it some unhealthy dependency and its consequent unhealthy demand. Let us, with God's help, continually surrender these hobbling liabilities."

———

From *The Language of the Heart*

AUGUST 2

"Responsibility Is Our Theme"

AA CO-FOUNDER, BILL W., JULY 1965

———

"Sometimes we register surprise, shock, and anger when people find fault with AA. We are apt to be disturbed to such an extent that we cannot benefit from constructive criticism. This sort of resentment makes no friends and achieves no constructive purpose. Certainly, this is an area in which we can improve."

———

From *The Language of the Heart*

AUGUST 3

"The Christmas Fighters"

QUOGUE, NEW YORK, DECEMBER 1963

———

"You never know until you go out
to meet it what any given day is going
to be, but the way you go to
meet it surely makes a difference."

———

From AA Grapevine

AUGUST 4

"Facing the Truth"

CLEVELAND, OHIO, FEBRUARY 1993

———

"I have had to face my past, one episode at a time, and become willing to look at the truth. I could feel the pain and fear, like trolls under the bridge, waiting to jump out and challenge my self-esteem."

———

From AA Grapevine

AUGUST 5

"Humility for Today"

AA CO-FOUNDER, BILL W., JUNE 1961

———

"Absolute humility would consist of a state of complete freedom from myself, freedom from all the claims that my defects of character now lay so heavily upon me. Perfect humility would be a full willingness, in all times and places, to find and to do the will of God."

———

From *The Language of the Heart*

AUGUST 6

"How Can Anyone Who Looks So Normal Be So Sick?"

JAMESTOWN, NEW YORK, APRIL 1992

———

"Some days I feel almost normal, almost sane."

———

From AA Grapevine

AUGUST 7

"Ripped Jeans and Threadbare High-Tops"

THE PAS, MANITOBA, JULY 1999

———

"I believe anyone can be helped
if they have an honest desire to stop
drinking. I'm living proof."

———

From *In Our Own Words*

AUGUST 8

"Caught in Hateland"

LA VERNE, CALIFORNIA, DECEMBER 1966

———

"I could do something about
changing my own thoughts,
but nothing about changing the
people around me."

———

From AA Grapevine

AUGUST 9

"Persons We Had Harmed"

REYNOLDSBURG, OHIO, SEPTEMBER 1979

———

"I do not need to make amends on my hands and knees; I need to walk tall, without false pride. When I go in humility and sincerely ask people to forgive me, this will remove the burden from my shoulders."

———

From AA Grapevine

AUGUST 10

"Short Takes"

HONOLULU, HAWAII, NOVEMBER 1962

———

"Habits are like cork or lead—they
tend to keep you up or hold
you down."

———

From AA Grapevine

AUGUST 11

"Listening and Learning"

PENNGROVE, CALIFORNIA, JANUARY 2008

———

"Alcoholism is relieved of its power when honesty, open-mindedness, and willingness combine within me to change my question from 'Why?' to 'How?' Then, I can get into the stream of life and out of my own way."

———

From AA Grapevine

AUGUST 12

"This Matter of Fear"

AA CO-FOUNDER, BILL W., JANUARY 1962

———

"We began to see adversity as a
God-given opportunity to develop
the kind of courage which is
born of humility, rather than bravado.
Thus we were enabled to accept
ourselves, our circumstances, and
our fellows."

———

From *The Best of Bill*

AUGUST 13

"An Unexpected Shot at Life"

PALMDALE, CALIFORNIA, JULY 1992

———

"I no longer always have to be right."

———

From AA Grapevine

AUGUST 14

"Leadership in AA: Ever a Vital Need"

AA CO-FOUNDER, BILL W., APRIL 1959

———

"Compromise comes hard to us 'all-or-nothing drunks.' Nevertheless, we must never lose sight of the fact that progress is nearly always characterized by *a series of improving compromises.*"

———

From *The Language of the Heart*

AUGUST 15

"Step Twelve: The Whole of AA"
COVENTRY, UNITED KINGDOM, DECEMBER 2007

———

"Putting principles before personalities, both inside and outside the Fellowship, does not always endear me to everyone, but I would rather be disliked for what I am than liked for what I am not."

———

From AA Grapevine

AUGUST 16

"A Really Good Idea"

SPRING CITY, UTAH, NOVEMBER 2003

———

"It's true that the only requirement
for membership in AA is a desire
to stop drinking. But if you absolutely
want a better life, well, hmmm. ...
How's this? Working the Steps with
a sponsor is a really good idea."

———

From AA Grapevine

AUGUST 17

"The Threat of the Twelve Steps"

VERMONT, OCTOBER 1965

———

"What is involved in taking the entire AA program, as the early AAs gave it to us, is not the prospect of turning into some sort of repulsive goody-goody. It's the threat of being truly alive, aware, and perhaps even ecstatic."

———

From AA Grapevine

AUGUST 18

"Let's Keep it Simple—But How?"

AA CO-FOUNDER, BILL W., JULY 1960

———

"There is among us AAs
the ever present need for further
spiritual growth."

———

From *The Language of the Heart*

AUGUST 19

"Service"

TACOMA, WASHINGTON, SEPTEMBER 1974

———

"It has only been in the past few months that I have become interested in service work in AA. Before that, I was an AA barnacle, glued to my seat, criticizing the speakers and griping about the coffee. Now I'm on the other side of the squawks and bleeps, and I find, to my delight, I like it."

———

From AA Grapevine

AUGUST 20

"Freedom Under God: The Choice Is Ours"

AA CO-FOUNDER, BILL W., NOVEMBER 1960

———

"The future would ... lack its full use and meaning did it not bring us fresh problems and even acute perils— problems and perils through which we can grow into true greatness of action and spirit."

———

From *The Language of the Heart*

AUGUST 21

"Savoring Our Sobriety"

NORTH HOLLYWOOD, CALIFORNIA, AUGUST 1982

———

"What counts is not that which can be held in the hand but that which can be held in the heart."

———

From *Emotional Sobriety*

AUGUST 22

"Boy Lying in the Grass"
ONTARIO, AUGUST 1962

———

"Grace is not a do-it-yourself project."

———

AUGUST 23

"Freedom Under God: The Choice Is Ours"

AA CO-FOUNDER, BILL W., NOVEMBER 1960

———

"We can achieve no liberation from the alcohol obsession until we become willing to deal with those character defects which have landed us in that helpless condition ... fear, anger, and pride ... rebellion and self-righteousness ... laziness and irresponsibility ... foolish rationalization and outright dishonesty ... wrong dependencies and destructive power-driving."

———

From *The Language of the Heart*

AUGUST 24

"Again at the Crossroads"

AA CO-FOUNDER, BILL W., NOVEMBER 1961

———

"In the nick of time, and by God's grace, each of us has been enabled to develop a growing sense of the meaning and purpose of his own life."

———

From *The Language of the Heart*

AUGUST 25

"8-½"

BOWLING GREEN, KENTUCKY, OCTOBER 1986

———

"My job is to achieve enough humility to see myself in others and to accept both myself and others, by identifying. The willingness to make amends will grow from this act of love."

———

AUGUST 26

"The Years That the Locust Hath Eaten"

NEW YORK, NEW YORK, APRIL 1997

———

"Forgiveness entered my life through my heart, not my head."

———

AUGUST 27

"This Business of Getting Ahead"
MANCHESTER, MASSACHUSETTS, OCTOBER 1964

———

"You cannot get ahead until you
learn to be here."

———

From AA Grapevine

AUGUST 28

"What Is Humility?"
MILWAUKEE, WISCONSIN, APRIL 1966

———

"Humility is the soil in which all
other virtues grow."

———

From AA Grapevine

AUGUST 29

"The Guy at the End of the Bar"

MARIETTA, OHIO, APRIL 1993

———

"It is impossible to know everyone,
but if I try to relate myself with just
one other person, something
will happen, something remarkable."

———

From AA Grapevine

AUGUST 30

"More Ups Than Downs"
NEW CANAAN, CONNECTICUT, JUNE 1974

———

"It's a wonderful feeling to know
that you don't have to be a god
or a goddess, a saint or a genius, to
lead a reasonably happy, sober,
healthy, communicative, constructive,
and useful life—with some
laughter thrown in for good measure."

———

From AA Grapevine

AUGUST 31

"Distilled Spirits"

TOBYHANNA, PENNSYLVANIA, JUNE 1995

———

"Don't regret growing old, it's a
privilege denied to many."

———

From AA Grapevine

SEPTEMBER

SEPTEMBER 1

"The Shape of Things to Come"

AA CO-FOUNDER, BILL W., FEBRUARY 1961

———

"We have to grow or else deteriorate. For us, the 'status quo' can only be for today, never for tomorrow. Change we must; we cannot stand still."

———

From *The Language of the Heart*

SEPTEMBER 2

"Savoring Our Sobriety"
NORTH HOLLYWOOD, CALIFORNIA, AUGUST 1982

———

"If we are to find spiritual growth and serenity, we must dress our minds each morning as carefully as we dress our bodies. Only then can today become the glorious tomorrow we looked forward to yesterday."

———

From *Emotional Sobriety*

SEPTEMBER 3

"Willingness to Grow"

JOLIET, ILLINOIS, JULY 1985

———

"Work on Step Nine has freed
me from fears about the
past and given me more energy
to devote to present-day
living—this twenty-four hours."

———

From AA Grapevine

SEPTEMBER 4

"Listen to People's Feelings"

GRANTS, NEW MEXICO, JULY 1980

———

"I spent years looking for things
to alienate me, make me different,
make me special or unique, better
or worse. ... I was taught through
the Steps to start dwelling
on the positive—the 'alikeness'
instead of the differences."

———

From *Young & Sober*

SEPTEMBER 5

"The Shape of Things to Come"

AA CO-FOUNDER, BILL W., FEBRUARY 1961

———

"Let us continue to take our inventory
as a Fellowship, searching out our
flaws and confessing them freely. Let
us devote ourselves to the repair
of all faulty relations that may exist,
whether within or without."

———

From *The Language of the Heart*

SEPTEMBER 6

"The Physicians"

AA CO-FOUNDER, BILL W., AUGUST 1957

"William Duncan Silkworth ... supplied us with the tools with which to puncture the toughest alcoholic ego, those shattering phrases by which he described our illness: *the obsession of the mind* that compels us to drink and *the allergy of the body* that condemns us to go mad or die. Without these indispensable passwords, AA could never have worked."

From *The Language of the Heart*

SEPTEMBER 7

"When I Was Sixteen, I Was Ready"

MAGNOLIA, ARKANSAS, JANUARY 1978

———

"I am glad for everything that has
happened to me. I have found a
way of life that I wouldn't trade for
anything in the world."

———

From *Young & Sober*

SEPTEMBER 8

"Surrender—Not Self-Improvement"

ATLANTA, GEORGIA, FEBRUARY 1990

———

"The amount of reality I turn my back
on is the amount I lose."

———

From *The Best of the Grapevine, Volume III*

SEPTEMBER 9

"Distilled Spirits"
INDIANAPOLIS, INDIANA, AUGUST 1982

———

"Humility is not thinking
less of yourself, but thinking
of yourself less."

———

From AA Grapevine

SEPTEMBER 10

"A Remarkable Sensation"

THOMPSON, PENNSYLVANIA, MARCH 1997

———

"Are you finally ready to let go
and live your destiny?"

———

From AA Grapevine

SEPTEMBER 11

"Teen Nightmare"

SAN JOSÉ, CALIFORNIA, OCTOBER 2011

———

"Whenever things get hard, or
I don't want to follow through
with a suggestion, I simply humble
myself to my Higher Power
and say, 'Just for today.' That helps
me live in the moment."

———

From Young & Sober

SEPTEMBER 12

"Distilled Spirits"

HERMOSA BEACH, CALIFORNIA, FEBRUARY 1998

———

"The number one way to relieve pain is to forgive."

———

From AA Grapevine

SEPTEMBER 13

"Responsibility Is Our Theme"

AA CO-FOUNDER, BILL W., JULY 1965

———

"Without much doubt, a million alcoholics have approached AA during the last thirty years. We can soberly ask ourselves what became of the 600,000 who did not stay."

———

From *The Language of the Heart*

SEPTEMBER 14

"Seventeen and Sober"

RICHMOND, NEW YORK, JANUARY 1978

———

"I'm learning to smile and laugh
again, and I've even gotten back some
of my self respect. ... I still have
problems, but AA has taught me how
to handle them and not to run
from them."

———

From *Young & Sober*

SEPTEMBER 15

"Leadership in AA: Ever a Vital Need"

AA CO-FOUNDER, BILL W., APRIL 1959

————

"Vision is ... the very essence of prudence."

————

From *The Language of the Heart*

SEPTEMBER 16

"Heard at Meetings"
JANUARY 1961

———

"When all else fails, try following
directions."

———

From AA Grapevine

SEPTEMBER 17

"The Hate-and-Pain Guy"
EUGENE, OREGON, JULY 2002

———

"Hope can be pretty damn contagious."

———

From *I Am Responsible*

SEPTEMBER 18

"The Key to Belonging"

MANCHESTER, NEW HAMPSHIRE,
SEPTEMBER 2000

———

"I discovered that there really is an easier, softer way—the way of striving to be a part of."

———

From *I Am Responsible*

SEPTEMBER 19

"Living Large"

SCHAUMBERG, ILLINOIS, MARCH 2006

———

"It took me a long time to find out that AA wasn't here to limit my life, it was here to fulfill it."

———

From Young & Sober

SEPTEMBER 20

"The Fundamentals in Retrospect"

AA CO-FOUNDER, DR. BOB, SEPTEMBER 1948

———

"The ego of the alcoholic dies a hard death ... fitting and wearing halos is not for us."

———

From *Spiritual Awakenings*

SEPTEMBER 21

"Nobody's Sweetheart"

MORENO VALLEY, CALIFORNIA, DECEMBER 1992

———

"My new friend asked when I had had my last drink, when I had eaten last, and if I was sleeping indoors that night. He told me his story. ... My hope was strengthened even more, and I knew I had found a way to live without booze."

———

From *I Am Responsible*

SEPTEMBER 22

"The Bill W. – Carl Jung Letters"

DR. C. G. JUNG, JANUARY 1963

———

"Alcohol in Latin is *spiritus*, and you use the same word for the highest religious experience as well as for the most depraving poison. The helpful formula therefore is: *spiritus contra spiritum.*"

———

From *The Language of the Heart*

SEPTEMBER 23

"Fountain of Youth"

NELSON, NEW HAMPSHIRE, AUGUST 1998

———

"I show up early, I am involved, and I reach my hand out to the next person coming though the door. It's amazing how very easy it is to make a difference for others and for yourself just by accepting the responsibility to pass the message on."

———

From *Young & Sober*

SEPTEMBER 24

"The Fundamentals in Retrospect"
AA CO-FOUNDER, DR. BOB, SEPTEMBER 1948

———

"Alcoholics Anonymous was nurtured in its early days around a kitchen table. ... True, we have progressed materially to better furniture and more comfortable surroundings. Yet the kitchen table must ever be appropriate for us. It is the perfect symbol of simplicity."

———

From *Spiritual Awakenings*

SEPTEMBER 25

"Fifth Tradition"

NEW YORK, NEW YORK, JUNE 1970

———

"I do not agree that the newcomer is the most important member at any meeting. ... Equally important are those old-timers who showed me the way, and any middle-timer who may be today suffering. If newcomers are indeed the lifeblood of AA, old- and middle-timers are its skin and backbone."

———

From I Am Responsible

SEPTEMBER 26

"More Than One Way"

CLEVELAND, OHIO, FEBRUARY 2010

———

"I have learned how to place
principles before personalities, begun
to understand that it's okay for
me to be wrong, and that it is also all
right for me to allow others to
be wrong and to make mistakes.
Learning to let go is a huge
part of service work on all levels."

———

From *Young & Sober*

SEPTEMBER 27

"Responsibility Is Our Theme"
AA CO-FOUNDER, BILL W., JULY 1965

———

"I have often seen our Society timid
and fearful, angry and prideful,
apathetic and indifferent. But I have
also seen these negatives fade
as the lessons of experience were
learned and gladly applied."

———

From *The Language of the Heart*

SEPTEMBER 28

"What Meeting Are You Going to Tomorrow?"

SANTA ROSA, CALIFORNIA, NOVEMBER 1999

———

"My recovery relies on the
hands of many people being extended
to me. The welcome I received
was more than a word. It was a word
followed by actions."

———

From *I Am Responsible*

SEPTEMBER 29

"So That's a Spiritual Experience!"

YORK, PENNSYLVANIA, JANUARY 1977

———

"I had been undergoing a spiritual experience without knowing it. My confused questioning about a Higher Power, my changed mental attitude, and even my physical recovery had all been part of a spiritual awakening. Without knowing it, I had been in contact with the source of life, whatever or Whoever that might be."

———

From *Spiritual Awakenings*

SEPTEMBER 30

"Distilled Spirits"
INDIANAPOLIS, INDIANA, AUGUST 1982

———

"Let today's troubles be sufficient
to today."

———

From AA Grapevine

OCTOBER

OCTOBER 1

"Wanted"

MANKATO, MINNESOTA, MAY 1997

———

"Life hasn't been all smooth sailing, but because of AA, I no longer have to live in fear. I sleep at night. ... I have a purpose in life."

———

From *Young & Sober*

OCTOBER 2

"Tradition Five"

AA CO-FOUNDER, BILL W., SEPTEMBER 1952

"The unique ability of each AA to identify himself with, and bring recovery to, the newcomer in no way depends upon his learning, eloquence, or on any special individual skills. The only thing that matters is that he is an alcoholic who has found a key to sobriety."

From AA Grapevine
(Reprinted in *Twelve Steps and Twelve Traditions*)

OCTOBER 3

"The Shape of Things to Come"

AA CO-FOUNDER, BILL W., FEBRUARY 1961

"Let us remember that great legion who still suffer from alcoholism and who are still without hope. Let us, at any cost or sacrifice, so improve our communication with all these that they may find what we have found— a new life of freedom under God."

From *I Am Responsible*

OCTOBER 4

"Not Under the Rug"
JANUARY 1967

———

"The more willing I become to admit it when I am wrong, the less often am I in the position of having to make such an admission."

———

From AA Grapevine

OCTOBER 5

"The Peace Process"

GOLD RIVER, CALIFORNIA, DECEMBER 1996

———

"I believe the peace I get from an effective Tenth Step is what God feels like."

———

From AA Grapevine

OCTOBER 6

"Listen to People's Feelings"

GRANTS, NEW MEXICO, JULY 1980

———

"I have a way to live that fills every
hole my gut ever had."

———

From *Young & Sober*

OCTOBER 7

"The Fundamentals in Retrospect"

AA CO-FOUNDER, DR. BOB, SEPTEMBER 1948

———

"In AA we have no VIPs, nor have we need of any. Our organization needs no title-holders nor grandiose buildings. ... Experience has taught us that simplicity is basic in preservation of our personal sobriety and helping those in need."

———

From *Spiritual Awakenings*

OCTOBER 8

"Leadership in AA: Ever a Vital Need"

AA CO-FOUNDER, BILL W., APRIL 1959

"A fine plan or idea can come from anybody, anywhere. Consequently, good leadership will often discard its own cherished plans for others that are better, and it will give credit to the source."

From *The Language of the Heart*

OCTOBER 9

"The Key to Belonging"

MANCHESTER, NEW HAMPSHIRE,
SEPTEMBER 2000

––––––

"What I've been willing to give to
AA, most often through my
home group, I've gotten back tenfold
in peace of mind."

––––––

From *I Am Responsible*

OCTOBER 10

"Distilled Spirits"
INDIANAPOLIS, INDIANA, AUGUST 1982

———

"Feed your faith and starve
your doubt."

———

From AA Grapevine

OCTOBER 11

"A Remarkable Sensation"

THOMPSON, PENNSYLVANIA, MARCH 1997

———

"As long as I am willing to do what I am called to do in any given moment and to abandon the effort to control the results of my actions, then I am following the path that my Higher Power—call it God, Good Orderly Direction, the soul, the life force, or anything else—has set out for me."

———

From AA Grapevine

OCTOBER 12

"Distilled Spirits"

INDIANAPOLIS, INDIANA, AUGUST 1982

———

"You don't help anyone by trying to impress them; you impress someone when you try to help them."

———

From AA Grapevine

OCTOBER 13

"Above All, an Alcoholic"

TOLEDO, OHIO, SEPTEMBER 1982

———

"By applying the principles of the program, I have gained my freedom— freedom to be myself, to like myself as I am, to become whatever it is that my Higher Power has planned for me, one day at a time— freedom to live the type of life I'm most comfortable with, to love, and to laugh."

———

From *In Our Own Words*

OCTOBER 14

"The Shape of Things to Come"

AA CO-FOUNDER, BILL W., FEBRUARY 1961

———

"While we need not alter our truths, we can surely improve their application to ourselves, to AA as a whole, and to our relation with the world around us. We can constantly step up 'the practice of these principles in all our affairs.'"

———

From *I Am Responsible*

OCTOBER 15

"It Might Have Been the Time..."
LOIS W., WIFE OF AA CO-FOUNDER BILL W.,
FEBRUARY 1950

———

"The fellowship in AA is unique. Ties
are made overnight that it would take
years to develop elsewhere. No one
needs a false front. All barriers are
down. Some who have felt outcasts all
their lives now know they really
belong. From feeling as if they were
dragging an anchor through life, they
suddenly sail free before the wind."

———

OCTOBER 16

"Distilled Spirits"
INDIANAPOLIS, INDIANA, AUGUST 1982

———

"It's hard to keep an open mind
with an open mouth."

———

From AA Grapevine

OCTOBER 17

"Distilled Spirits"
INDIANAPOLIS, INDIANA, AUGUST 1982

———

"Complaining is not an action step."

———

From AA Grapevine

OCTOBER 18

"The Gift of Time"

DOVER, PENNSYLVANIA, JUNE 1991

———

"I was told that sometimes a good
sponsor disturbs the comfortable and
comforts the disturbed."

———

From *In Our Own Words*

OCTOBER 19

"Slips and Human Nature"

WILLIAM DUNCAN SILKWORTH, MD,
JANUARY 1947

———

"There is a tendency to label everything that an alcoholic may do as 'alcoholic behavior.' The truth is, it is simply human nature. ... Emotional and mental quirks are classified as symptoms of alcoholism merely because alcoholics have them, yet those same quirks can be found among nonalcoholics, too. Actually they are symptoms of mankind."

———

From *The Best of the Grapevine, Volume I*

OCTOBER 20

"Services Make AA Tick"

AA CO-FOUNDER, BILL W., NOVEMBER 1951

———

"We saw we'd have to have service committees or fail to function, perhaps fall apart entirely. We'd actually *have to organize services in order to Keep AA Simple.*"

———

From *The Language of the Heart*

OCTOBER 21

"Why Alcoholics Anonymous Is Anonymous"

AA CO-FOUNDER, BILL W., JANUARY 1955

———

"At the beginning we sacrificed alcohol. We had to, or it would have killed us. But we couldn't get rid of alcohol unless we made other sacrifices. Big shot-ism and phony thinking had to go. We had to toss self-justification, self-pity, and anger right out the window. We had to quit the crazy contest for personal prestige and big bank balances. We had to take personal responsibility for our sorry state and quit blaming others for it."

———

From *The Language of the Heart*

OCTOBER 22

"Together We Can"

MARTINSVILLE, WEST VIRGINIA, JANUARY 1990

———

"Talking about what bothers me
helps it lose its power over me."

———

OCTOBER 23

"A Long Way Down"

ARLINGTON, TEXAS, JULY 1994

———

"I'm learning to be a mother, a friend, a grandmother, and a sister. My friends are a close-knit support group, and they're as near as the telephone."

———

OCTOBER 24

"Love"

NORTH HOLLYWOOD, CALIFORNIA,
SEPTEMBER 1988

———

"When we love, we will see in others
what we wish to see in ourselves."

———

From *The Best of the Grapevine, Volume III*

OCTOBER 25

"Ph. Drunk"

GREENSBORO, NORTH CAROLINA,
FEBRUARY 1987

———

"Pride in my intelligence blinded me
to how much I did not know."

———

OCTOBER 26

"Truth"

KEY WEST, FLORIDA, AUGUST 1973

———

"Truth is not a bludgeon to be used
indiscriminately. ... When I am asked
for an opinion or advice, I give it
to the best of my ability with as much
gentleness, understanding,
and tolerance as I can scrape up."

———

From *The Best of the Grapevine, Volume I*

OCTOBER 27

"Tradition Ten"

NEW YORK, NEW YORK, MAY 1971

———

"We all know whose inventory we
take in AA, right?"

———

OCTOBER 28

"Keep Coming Back—No Matter What"

SALT LAKE CITY, UTAH, NOVEMBER 2000

———

"I have no idea how I made it this long, or what has kept me sober. But if I were to guess, I'd say that it has something to do with the slogan, 'Keep coming back—no matter what.'"

———

From *In Our Own Words*

OCTOBER 29

"Service Is the Reason"
WINNIPEG, MANITOBA, JUNE 1979

———

"I can no longer use the illness of alcoholism as an excuse for anything. There is a catch, however. If I fail to use my recovery in service to others, I will become sick again."

———

From *The Best of the Grapevine, Volume II*

OCTOBER 30

"No Longer Alone"

FLUSHING, NEW YORK, MARCH 1995

———

"I've found the comfort, love,
and support I need to pick up the
pieces and try again after
my setbacks. ... I'm not alone in
my journey."

———

OCTOBER 31

"Life Is Meant to Be Lived"

SPRING HILL, FLORIDA, SEPTEMBER 1985

———

"There are more amends to be made,
letters to be sent, Twelfth Step
work to be done, responsibilities to be
assumed, and honest talks to be
had with loved ones. Life is meant to
be lived by facing the challenges
it brings. Otherwise, I'm not living,
just existing."

———

From *The Best of the Grapevine, Volume III*

NOVEMBER

NOVEMBER 1

"Sobriety for Ourselves"

NEW YORK, NEW YORK, NOVEMBER 1946

———

"Laughter is one of God's greatest
and most beneficent gifts to us. Laugh
with him sometimes at yourself."

———

From *Thank You for Sharing*

NOVEMBER 2

Editorial

AA CO-FOUNDER, BILL W., NOVEMBER 1958

———

"Suffering is no longer a menace to be evaded at any cost. When it does come, no matter how grievously, we realize that it too has its purpose. It is our great teacher because it reveals our defects and so pushes us forward into the paths of progress. The pain of drinking did just this for us. And so can any other pain."

———

From AA Grapevine

NOVEMBER 3

"Short Takes"

MAY 1953

———

"Happiness is not a station we arrive at; it's a way of traveling."

———

NOVEMBER 4

"Charming Is the Word for Alcoholics"

FULTON OURSLER, FRIEND OF AA, JULY 1944

———

"I number among my friends stars and lesser lights of stage and cinema; writers are my daily diet; I know the ladies and gentlemen of both political parties; I have been entertained in the White House; I have broken bread with kings and ministers and ambassadors; and I say, after that catalog, that I would prefer an evening with my AA friends to an evening with any person or group of persons I have indicated."

———

From *The Best of the Grapevine, Volume I*

NOVEMBER 5

"Meetings, Meetings, Meetings"
GRAND RAPIDS, MICHIGAN, OCTOBER 1981

———

"The best way to appreciate
AA is the same way you
appreciate a stained-glass window:
Look at it from the inside."

———

From *Happy, Joyous and Free*

NOVEMBER 6

"Why Alcoholics Anonymous Is Anonymous"

AA CO-FOUNDER, BILL W., JANUARY 1955

———

"We can, through broken anonymity, resume our old and disastrous pursuit of personal power and prestige, public honors, and money— the same implacable urges that when frustrated once caused us to drink; the same forces that are today ripping the globe apart at its seams."

———

From *The Language of the Heart*

NOVEMBER 7

"Meetings, Meetings, Meetings"
GRAND RAPIDS, MICHIGAN, OCTOBER 1981

———

"When I was drinking, I was
afraid I was not achieving
my potential. Now that I'm sober,
I worry that maybe I am."

———

From *Happy, Joyous and Free*

NOVEMBER 8

"Sobriety for Ourselves"

NEW YORK, NEW YORK, NOVEMBER 1946

———

"To know yourself is not done just by reviewing your 'misdeeds'; they are not you. ... Your doubts, fears, and apprehensions, your immature cravings, your self-indulgence ... they are all committed by your physical body, guided by false instincts and imagination, instead of by your real self, which is the soul—the spirit within. That is where your conscience is, and your wisdom and your strength—which no one can hurt but you."

———

From *Thank You for Sharing*

NOVEMBER 9

"Blessed with the Memory of My Pain"

KENNER, LOUISIANA, JANUARY 1996

———

"Things haven't been all roses but they are certainly not comparable to the way they were. God has blessed me with a vivid memory of my pain, which has helped me ... when the thought of escaping popped into my head."

———

From *Young & Sober*

NOVEMBER 10

"Under New Management"

COLLEGE PARK, MARYLAND, JUNE 1982

———

"I realize now that most of the problems in my life were a direct result of my attempts to handle my own life, to be in control of my own destiny. I am grateful that today, sober, I can still say my life has 'become unmanageable.'"

———

From *Spiritual Awakenings*

NOVEMBER 11

"Beyond the Generation Gap"
SARATOGA, CALIFORNIA, AUGUST 1985

———

"Let us not be afraid of unsettling
or boring our comrades by
talking about our reactions to
whatever is bothering us at a
given moment; for this is how
we learn to live."

———

From *The Home Group*

NOVEMBER 12

"On Cultivating Tolerance"

AA CO-FOUNDER, DR. BOB, JULY 1944

———

"Tolerance ... promotes an open-mindedness that is vastly important —is, in fact, a prerequisite to the successful termination of any line of search, whether it be scientific or spiritual."

———

NOVEMBER 13

"Just a Drunk"

AURORA, ILLINOIS, AUGUST 1992

———

"I pray that I will stay humble and not forget that I am just a drunk, sober today through the grace of God and the program of AA."

———

From AA Grapevine

NOVEMBER 14

"Alcoholism and Alcoholics Anonymous"

MARVIN A. BLOCK, MD, FRIEND OF AA,
FEBRUARY 1974

———

"Once the alcoholic understands the desirability of accepting reality, to the best of his ability and within the limits which we all have, he has taken a step toward maturity. The difference between the mentally healthy person and the unhealthy one is the ability to face the realities of life."

———

From *I Am Responsible*

NOVEMBER 15

"Practical Enlightenment"
SAN FRANCISCO, CALIFORNIA, AUGUST 1995

———

"Open-mindedness seems
to me a core spiritual principle
of the program. ...
Without it I cannot change."

———

From *Spiritual Awakenings*

NOVEMBER 16

"Faith Is Action"

CULVER CITY, CALIFORNIA, MAY 1977

———

"Whether I conceive of God as a set of immutable cosmic laws or as an old man with a white robe and matching beard is totally and gloriously irrelevant. All that matters are my values and attitudes and how I act upon them."

———

From *Spiritual Awakenings*

NOVEMBER 17

"Nobody's Sweetheart"
MORENO VALLEY, CALIFORNIA, DECEMBER 1992

———

"It has been the actions of others that has given me unfailing support throughout my sobriety. It also shows how I am to respond to those whom I can help. I am responsible to see that the hand of AA is available to anyone."

———

From *I Am Responsible*

NOVEMBER 18

"The Light in the Window"

LAKE WORTH, FLORIDA, JUNE 1999

———

"It isn't possible for all of us to be loners."

———

From *I Am Responsible*

NOVEMBER 19

"The Old Fear Had to Go"

BINGHAMTON, NEW YORK, APRIL 1968

———

"In AA's Eleventh Step I find
that I build today the road I travel
tomorrow."

———

From AA Grapevine

NOVEMBER 20

"AA Is Not Big Business"

AA CO-FOUNDER, BILL W., NOVEMBER 1950

———

"We've resolved never to allow either money or the management of our necessary affairs to obscure our spiritual aims."

———

From *The Language of the Heart*

NOVEMBER 21

"Prayer"

SEATTLE, WASHINGTON, APRIL 1974

———

"The emotional balance that eluded me is returning with prayer."

———

From *Spiritual Awakenings*

NOVEMBER 22

"Tradition Seven"

AA CO-FOUNDER, BILL W., JUNE 1948

———

"Yes, we AAs were once a burden on everybody. We were 'takers.' Now that we are sober, and by the grace of God have become responsible citizens of the world, why shouldn't we now about-face and become 'thankful givers'! Yes, it is high time we did!"

———

From *The Language of the Heart*

NOVEMBER 23

"Trusting the Silence"

NOVEMBER 1991

———

"My prayers are usually brief and to the point. 'Help!' is one I use often."

———

NOVEMBER 24

"Just Keep On Going"

NEW CANAAN, CONNECTICUT, APRIL 1976

———

"I know that I am not a total loss, even when I think I am. I know that freedom and usefulness, love, outgoingness, and sharing are the important things in life."

———

NOVEMBER 25

"Back from Haiti"

IOWA CITY, IOWA, AUGUST 2012

———

"I know that I will never be sober long enough to be alcohol-proof."

———

From AA Grapevine

NOVEMBER 26

"Nobody's Fault but Mine"
NIPAWIN, SASKATCHEWAN, NOVEMBER 2003

———

"After so many years of being
a hazard, a public nuisance
at best, I feel obliged
to do something positive."

———

From *Happy, Joyous and Free*

NOVEMBER 27

"Another Hand to Help Me Along"

ALLYN, WASHINGTON, FEBRUARY 1997

———

"There is always grace for the
days I'm helpless."

———

NOVEMBER 28

"Thanks America!"

NEW YORK, AUGUST 2012

———

"I went to Paris when I was young to become an artist. I wanted to be rich and famous, but God had another plan. I'm neither rich nor famous. Instead, I got sober."

———

From AA Grapevine

NOVEMBER 29

"Gratitude"

NEW CANAAN, CONNECTICUT, SEPTEMBER 1979

———

"Don't wait till you're depressed
to practice gratitude."

———

From *Voices of Long-Term Sobriety*

NOVEMBER 30

"The Need to Go Deeper"
SHREVEPORT, LOUISIANA, AUGUST 2012

———

"As I continue to see the
inherent worth and dignity in every
human being, I will continue
to live on a more level playing field
with everybody."

———

From AA Grapevine

DECEMBER

DECEMBER 1

"Then Came Susan and Dottie"

ELKTON, MARYLAND, AUGUST 2012

———

"Living sober is not all roses all the time. But the cool thing is, when I am nervous, it is OK. I do not have to drink to fix it. It is the same with being sad, worried or afraid."

———

From AA Grapevine

DECEMBER 2

"Just Keep On Going"
NEW CANAAN, CONNECTICUT, APRIL 1976

———

"Thank God for all the wonderful people, professional and otherwise, who have helped me or tried to. Even when the help has not succeeded, it has kept me going, kept me trying."

———

DECEMBER 3

"This Matter of Honesty"

AA CO-FOUNDER, BILL W., AUGUST 1961

———

"When life presents us with a racking conflict ... we cannot be altogether blamed if we are confused. In fact, our very first responsibility is to admit that we *are* confused."

———

From *The Language of the Heart*

DECEMBER 4

"Truth"

KEY WEST, FLORIDA, AUGUST 1973

———

"Truth is not an immutable absolute,
a granite peak, eternal, unmoving,
hiding its head in a nimbus of clouds.
Truth is a ballerina tracing
arabesques in a pattern of color and
music, ever-changing, harmonious."

———

DECEMBER 5

"Caught in Hateland"
LA VERNE, CALIFORNIA, DECEMBER 1966

———

"The most important factor in
eliminating resentments
is to know you have them. You
can't fix something if
you don't know what's wrong."

———

DECEMBER 6

"Services Make AA Tick"

AA CO-FOUNDER, BILL W., NOVEMBER 1951

"By 1937, some of us realized that AA needed a standard literature. There would have to be a book. ... Well, we did quarrel violently over the preparation and distribution of that book. In fact, it took five years for the clamor to die down. Should any AAs dream that the old-timers who put the book together went about in serene meditation and white robes, then they had best forget it."

From *The Language of the Heart*

DECEMBER 7

"Ever Been on a Dry Drunk?"

DAYTON, OHIO, APRIL 1962

———

"There have been dark days where a will infinitely greater than my own has been responsible for my sobriety."

———

From *The Best of the Grapevine, Volume I*

DECEMBER 8

"What I Learned from My Sponsor"

AUSTIN, TEXAS, MAY 2003

———

"The reason we try to carry the
message is so that we stay sober.
If the person we are helping
stays sober, that's an extra bonus."

———

DECEMBER 9

"Those Depressions—Make Them Work for Good!"

NEW YORK, NEW YORK, AUGUST 1948

———

"If we can stop this frantic drive to prove that we are remarkable people, it is quite likely that we will settle down and really enjoy whatever life has to offer us."

———

DECEMBER 10

"The Next Frontier: Emotional Sobriety"

AA CO-FOUNDER, BILL W., JANUARY 1958

———

"Happiness is a by-product—the extra dividend of giving without any demand for a return."

———

From *The Language of the Heart*

DECEMBER 11

"How AA Works"

SANTA FE, NEW MEXICO, MAY 1972

———

"When you've been lost, lonely,
forgotten, rejected, it's the most
important thing in the world
to have somebody shake your hand."

———

DECEMBER 12

"Tradition One"

NEW YORK, NEW YORK, NOVEMBER 1969

———

"The simple act of getting in touch
with AA that first time washed
out in an instant the dark loneliness
that had encompassed my life."

———

From *The Best of the Grapevine, Volume I*

DECEMBER 13

"Don't Hide in AA"

FOREST HILLS, NEW YORK, JANUARY 1967

———

"Neither God nor AA can help us if
we are not open to help."

———

DECEMBER 14

"What Is Acceptance?"

AA CO-FOUNDER, BILL W., MARCH 1962

———

"Life's formidable array of pains and problems will require many different degrees of acceptance. ... Sometimes, we have to find the right kind of acceptance for each day. Sometimes, we need to develop acceptance for what may come to pass tomorrow and, yet again, we shall have to accept a condition that may never change. Then, too, there frequently has to be a right and realistic acceptance of grievous flaws within ourselves and serious faults within those about us—defects that may not be fully remedied for years, if ever."

———

From *The Language of the Heart*

DECEMBER 15

"What About This 24-Hour Plan?"

NEW YORK, NEW YORK, JANUARY 1968

———

"With a recovering alcoholic,
action has to come before
understanding and faith. ... We
have to act our way to right
thinking, rather than the reverse."

———

DECEMBER 16

"After the Fall"

SPARKS, NEVADA, AUGUST 1969

———

"I must continue to see
my own kinship with whatever
God is identifiable, just as
relentlessly as I work to make
each minute a sober one."

———

DECEMBER 17

"Slips and Human Nature"

WILLIAM DUNCAN SILKWORTH, MD,
JANUARY 1947

———

"The alcoholic slip is not a symptom of a psychotic condition. There's nothing screwy about it at all. *The patient simply didn't follow directions.*"

———

DECEMBER 18

"Tradition Two"

NEW YORK, NEW YORK, DECEMBER 1969

———

"It has to be love, not government
that keeps AA stuck together."

———

DECEMBER 19

"Accepting the Invitation"
OKMULGEE, OKLAHOMA, MAY 1994

———

"I accepted the invitation to go
on a Twelfth Step call and I in turn
was twelfth-stepped."

———

From *I Am Responsible*

DECEMBER 20

"Remembering a Girl—Defeated Except Once"

ARLINGTON, VIRGINIA, MARCH 1947

———

"I am grateful for this minute.
My eternity may be in it."

———

DECEMBER 21

"Ever Been on a Dry Drunk?"

DAYTON, OHIO, APRIL 1962

———

"No one can express love and self-pity at the same moment; showing concern for others helps us to see how foolish we have been."

———

From *The Best of the Grapevine, Volume I*

DECEMBER 22

"This Matter of Honesty"

AA CO-FOUNDER, BILL W., AUGUST 1961

"We cannot wholly rely on friends to solve all our difficulties. A good adviser will never do all our thinking for us. He knows that each final choice must be ours."

From *The Language of the Heart*

DECEMBER 23

"Respecting Money"

AA CO-FOUNDER, BILL W., NOVEMBER 1957

———

"Our spiritual way of life is safe for future generations if, as a Society, we resist the temptation to receive money from the outside world. But this leaves us with a responsibility— one that every member ought to understand. We cannot skimp when the treasurer of our group passes the hat. Our groups, our areas, and AA as a whole will not function unless our services are sufficient and their bills are paid."

———

From *The Language of the Heart*

DECEMBER 24

"Self-Pity Can Kill"

KEY WEST, FLORIDA, FEBRUARY 1973

———

"Do I really want ... to be bitter, hostile, and judgmental? Do I want to live inside that sort of person? Wouldn't I rather forgive, make allowances, understand? Is self-pity, feeling abused, so precious that I will not trade it for self-liking?"

———

From *The Best of the Grapevine, Volume I*

DECEMBER 25

"A Christmas Message"

AA CO-FOUNDER, BILL W., DECEMBER 1970

———

"Gratitude is just about the finest
attribute we can have."

———

From *The Language of the Heart*

DECEMBER 26

"The Vision of Tomorrow"
AA CO-FOUNDER, BILL W., JANUARY 1952

———

"Clear vision for tomorrow comes only after a real look at yesterday."

———

From *The Language of the Heart*

DECEMBER 27

"The Fear of Feeling Rejected"

VENICE, CALIFORNIA, OCTOBER 1973

———

"I persist in the face of defeat. I can risk being rejected now, because I no longer have to feel resentful and depressed when it happens."

———

DECEMBER 28

"Ever Been on a Dry Drunk?"

DAYTON, OHIO, APRIL 1962

———

"The emotions of an alcoholic
can fluctuate much in the manner
of weather fronts."

———

DECEMBER 29

"... And Learn"

ORANGE, CALIFORNIA, NOVEMBER 1996

———

"By working with others I'm allowed to witness the miracle of sobriety and observe the twinkling eyes as others learn to speak the language of the heart."

———

From AA Grapevine

DECEMBER 30

"Self-Pity Can Kill"

KEY WEST, FLORIDA, FEBRUARY 1973

———

"As drinking alcoholics, we all ran from life and toward death. When we join AA, we reverse the process— we give ourselves to life as it is, rather than as we would like it to be."

———

DECEMBER 31

"Those Depressions—Make Them Work for Good!"

NEW YORK, NEW YORK, AUGUST 1948

———

"There is one job that we can
do superlatively well, and there isn't
anything that can keep us from
doing it if we are serious in wanting
to. That is the job we do on
ourselves, inside ourselves. It means
clearing out a whole mess of false
values, unrealistic ambitions, and
worn-out resentments, and putting in
their place the qualities we
want to have—kindness, tolerance,
friendliness. ... We can begin to
see what the real values of life are,
and they are very different from
the hazy, distorted dreams we had."

———

From *The Best of the Grapevine, Volume I*

THE TWELVE STEPS

1. We admitted we were powerless over alcohol—that our lives had become unmanageable.

2. Came to believe that a Power greater than ourselves could restore us to sanity.

3. Made a decision to turn our will and our lives over to the care of God *as we understood Him.*

4. Made a searching and fearless moral inventory of ourselves.

5. Admitted to God, to ourselves, and to another human being the exact nature of our wrongs.

6. Were entirely ready to have God remove all these defects of character.

7. Humbly asked Him to remove our shortcomings.

8. Made a list of all persons we had harmed, and became willing to make amends to them all.

9. Made direct amends to such people wherever possible, except when to do so would injure them or others.

10. Continued to take personal inventory and when we were wrong promptly admitted it.

11. Sought through prayer and meditation to improve our conscious contact with God *as we understood Him,* praying only for knowledge of His will for us and the power to carry that out.

12. Having had a spiritual awakening as the result of these steps, we tried to carry this message to alcoholics, and to practice these principles in all our affairs.

THE TWELVE TRADITIONS

1. Our common welfare should come first; personal recovery depends upon A.A. unity.

2. For our group purpose there is but one ultimate authority—a loving God as He may express Himself in our group conscience. Our leaders are but trusted servants; they do not govern.

3. The only requirement for A.A. membership is a desire to stop drinking.

4. Each group should be autonomous except in matters affecting other groups or A.A. as a whole.

5. Each group has but one primary purpose—to carry its message to the alcoholic who still suffers.

6. An A.A. group ought never endorse, finance or lend the A.A. name to any related facility or outside enterprise, lest problems of money, property and prestige divert us from our primary purpose.

7. Every A.A. group ought to be fully self-supporting, declining outside contributions.

8. Alcoholics Anonymous should remain forever nonprofessional, but our service centers may employ special workers.

9. A.A., as such, ought never be organized; but we may create service boards or committees directly responsible to those they serve.

10. Alcoholics Anonymous has no opinion on outside issues; hence the A.A. name ought never be drawn into public controversy.

11. Our public relations policy is based on attraction rather than promotion; we need always maintain personal anonymity at the level of press, radio and films.

12. Anonymity is the spiritual foundation of all our traditions, ever reminding us to place principles before personalities.

ALCOHOLICS ANONYMOUS

AA's program of recovery is fully set forth in its basic text, *Alcoholics Anonymous* (commonly known as the Big Book), now in its Fourth Edition, as well as in *Twelve Steps and Twelve Traditions*, *Living Sober*, and other books. Information on AA can also be found on AA's website at www.AA.ORG, or by writing to:

Alcoholics Anonymous
Box 459
Grand Central Station
New York, NY 10163

For local resources, check your local telephone directory under "Alcoholics Anonymous." Four pamphlets, "This is A.A.," "Is A.A. For You?," "44 Questions," and "A Newcomer Asks" are also available from AA.

AA GRAPEVINE

AA Grapevine is AA's international monthly journal, published continuously since its first issue in June 1944. The AA pamphlet on AA Grapevine describes its scope and purpose this way: "As an integral part of Alcoholics Anonymous for more than sixty years, Grapevine publishes articles that reflect the full diversity of experience and thought found within the AA Fellowship. No one viewpoint or philosophy dominates its pages, and in determining content, the editorial staff relies on the principles of the Twelve Traditions." AA Grapevine also publishes La Viña, AA's Spanish-language print magazine, which serves the Hispanic AA community.

In addition to magazines, AA Grapevine, Inc. also produces books, eBooks, audiobooks, and other items. It also offers a Grapevine Online subscription, which includes: five new stories weekly, AudioGrapevine (the audio version of the magazine), Grapevine Story Archive (the entire collection of Grapevine articles), and the current issue of Grapevine and La Viña in HTML format. For more information on AA Grapevine, or to subscribe to any of these, please visit the magazine's website at www.AAGRAPEVINE.ORG or write to:

AA Grapevine, Inc.
475 Riverside Drive
New York, NY 10115

INDEX